SUPER SCRATCH PROGRAMMING ADVENTURE!

LEARN TO PROGRAM BY MAKING COOL GAMES!

Super Scratch Programming Adventure! is a translation of the original Traditional Chinese–language edition, *Easy LEAD* 創意程式設計 *Scratch* 遊俠傳 (*Easy LEAD: The Scratch Musketeers*), ISBN 978-988-18408-2-0, published by the Hong Kong Federation of Youth Groups, © 2010 by the Hong Kong Federation of Youth Groups.

Printed in Canada

First printing

15 14 13 12   1 2 3 4 5 6 7 8 9

ISBN-10: 1-59327-409-2
ISBN-13: 978-1-59327-409-2

Publisher: William Pollock
Adviser: Dr. Rosanna Wong Yick-ming, DBE, JP
Editorial Team: Yolanda Chiu, Alice Lui, Edmond Kim Ping Hui
Contributors: Edmond Kim Ping Hui (Book Contents); Man Chun Chow, Chun Hei Tse, Vincent Wong (Assistance & Photography)
Interior Design: LOL Design Ltd.
Production Editor: Serena Yang
Cover Design: Sonia Brown
Developmental Editor: Tyler Ortman
Technical Reviewer: Michael Smith-Welch
Copyeditor: Marilyn Smith
Compositor: Riley Hoffman
Proofreader: Serena Yang

For information on book distributors or translations, please contact No Starch Press, Inc. directly:

No Starch Press, Inc.
38 Ringold Street, San Francisco, CA 94103
phone: 415.863.9900; fax: 415.863.9950; info@nostarch.com; http://www.nostarch.com/

Library of Congress Cataloging-in-Publication Data
A catalog record of this book is available from the Library of Congress.

CONTENTS

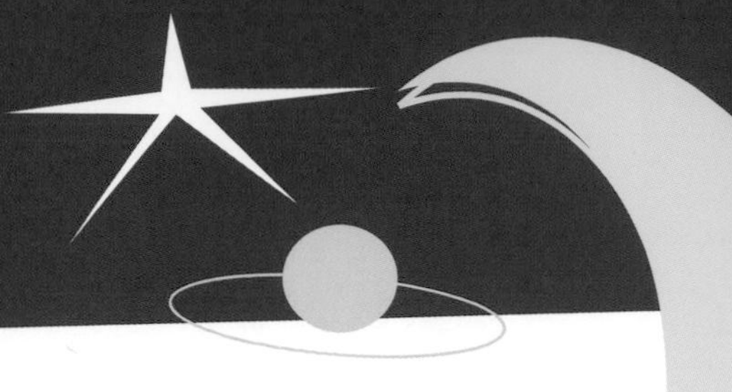

FOREWORD

Scratch is more than a piece of software. It is part of a broader educational mission. We designed Scratch to help young people prepare for life in today's fast-changing society. As young people create Scratch projects, they are not just learning how to write computer programs. They are learning to think creatively, reason systematically, and work collaboratively—essential skills for success and happiness in today's world.

It has been exciting to see all of the creative ways that young people are using Scratch. On the Scratch website (*http://scratch.mit.edu/*), young people from around the world are sharing a wide variety of creative projects: animated stories, adventure games, interactive tutorials, guided tours, science experiments, online newsletters, and much more. Scratch is a digital sandbox where young people can express themselves creatively—and, in the process, develop as creative thinkers.

Super Scratch Programming Adventure! will help introduce more young people to the creative possibilities of Scratch. The book grows out of one of the world's most innovative and productive Scratch initiatives, organized by the Hong Kong Federation of Youth Groups. I'm delighted that their ideas and activities are now available to teachers, parents, and children around the world.

As you read this book, let your imagination run wild. What will you create with Scratch?

Enjoy the adventure!

Mitchel Resnick

Professor Mitchel Resnick
Director, MIT Scratch Team
MIT Media Lab

A NOTE OF THANKS

The Hong Kong Federation of Youth Groups created the Learning through Engineering, Art and Design (LEAD) Project in 2005 in collaboration with the MIT Media Lab and the Chinese University of Hong Kong. The LEAD Project promotes hands-on, design-based activities with the creative use of technology and aims to develop an innovative spirit among the youth of Hong Kong. Since its founding, it has promoted technology education on a grand scale, reaching more than 1,000,000 students, parents, and educators.

Super Scratch Programming Adventure! is our second of three books about Scratch and the first to be translated into English. This book highlights the playful spirit of learning to program with Scratch, which inspires young people to apply digital technologies in imaginative and innovative ways.

We are very grateful to the MIT Media Lab, which has been our partner since LEAD was established in 2005. We are particularly appreciative of Professor Mitchel Resnick and Mr. Michael Smith-Welch, who have always been LEAD's staunchest supporters and greatest cheerleaders. Because of their unwavering belief in Scratch and in LEAD, you are now able to read this English edition.

We hope this book inspires you to design your very own games, projects, and more with Scratch.

Dr. Rosanna Wong Yick-ming, DBE, JP
Executive Director
The Hong Kong Federation of Youth Groups

A NOTE FOR PARENTS AND EDUCATORS

Scratch opens up an exciting world of computer programming for kids and other beginning programmers. The *most* technical part of using Scratch may actually be installing the program.

To follow along with this book, you'll need Scratch installed on your computer and the project files for the games.

- Download Scratch 1.4 from *http://scratch.mit.edu/* and follow the installation instructions for your operating system. Scratch runs on Windows, Mac, and Linux computers. Try running Scratch to make sure your installation was successful.
- Download the projects for this book from *http://nostarch.com/scratch/*. This online resource includes complete projects, custom sprites, and a short *Getting Started With Scratch* guide. Place the project files within the *Scratch* folder so you can find them easily.

  The *Resources* file includes two versions of each game in the book. One version is a completely finished and playable game, perfect for young learners and anyone who wants to build on the games in the book. The second set of projects has no programming added, so that students can follow along with the programming instructions in this book. Remember, there's no wrong way to play with Scratch!

WHAT IS SCRATCH, ANYWAY?

Scratch is a graphical programming language that you can download for free. By simply dragging and dropping colored blocks, you can create interactive stories, games, animation, music, art, and presentations. You can even upload your creations to the Internet to share with others from around the world. Scratch is designed for play, self-learning, and design.

WHERE DID THE NAME SCRATCH COME FROM?

Scratch is named for the way that hip-hop disc jockeys (DJs) creatively combine pieces of music, using a technique called *scratching*. In the same way, programmers in Scratch join different media (images, photos, sound effects, and so on) together in exciting ways to create something entirely new.

WHO CREATED SCRATCH?

Scratch is a project funded by the US National Science Foundation (NSF). It was developed by the Massachusetts Institute of Technology (MIT) Media Lab's Lifelong Kindergarten Group.

WHO IS SCRATCH FOR?

Scratch was developed for young people aged 8 and up to develop creative learning skills for the twenty-first century. When they create programs, they learn important mathematical

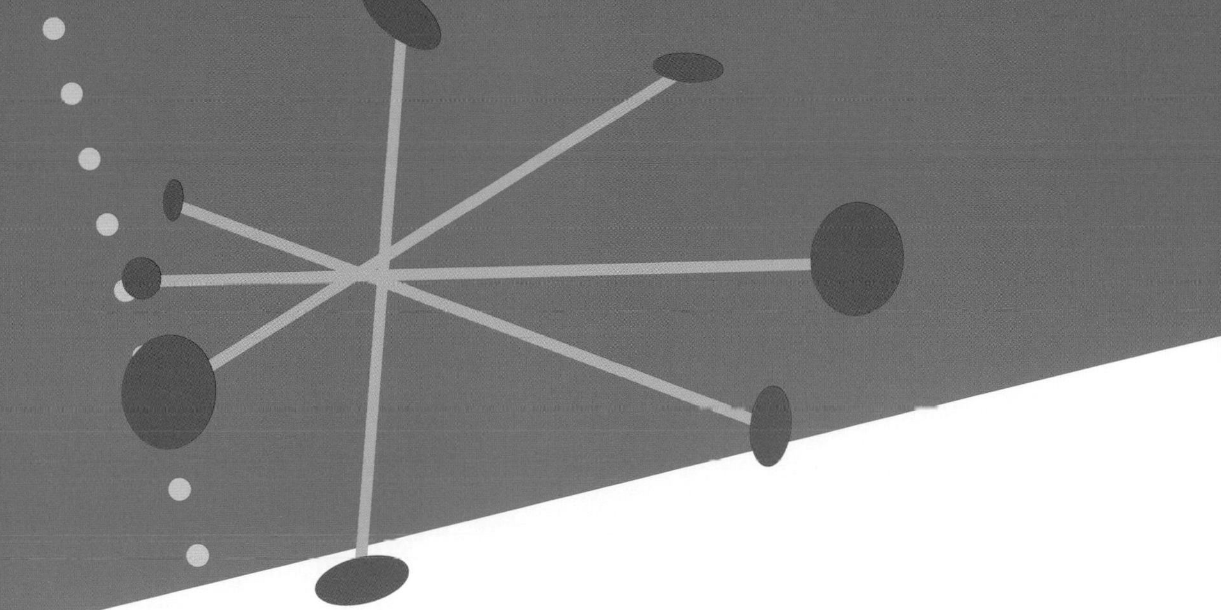

and computer concepts that improve their creative thinking, logical reasoning, problem solving, and collaboration skills.

Designing Scratch projects challenges creative thinking skills, and overcoming obstacles and problem solving builds confidence. This gives learners an advantage later in life.

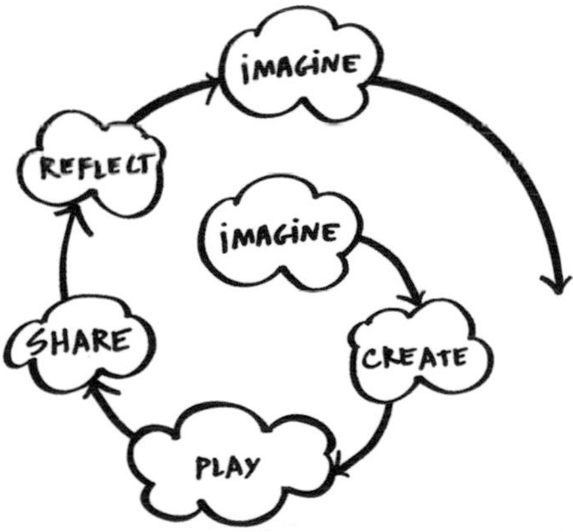

This creative thinking spiral is from Professor Resnick's article, "Sowing the Seeds of a More Creative Society," published in *ISTE (International Society for Technology in Education).*

IS IT EASY TO USE SCRATCH?

Scratch was designed to prevent common beginner pitfalls like misspelling and errors in consistency. Instead of typing commands, programming in Scratch is performed by dragging and joining programming blocks. This graphical interface allows users to easily control the way different types of commands react

together. Additionally, each block can fit with another only if it makes computational sense. Colorized categories help organize and group different sets of related commands based on their particular function.

Since programs in Scratch run in real time, programs can be edited and tested at any given moment, *even while the program is running*. This allows users to easily experiment with new ideas or to repeatedly test their improvements!

HOW MANY LANGUAGES DOES SCRATCH SUPPORT?

Scratch can be used in 50 different languages. Just click the globe to change the active language in the program.

WHERE CAN YOU USE SCRATCH?

You can use Scratch at schools, libraries, community centers, and home. Even though Scratch is designed for young people aged 8 and up, younger children can also learn to design and create alongside their parents or siblings.

Scratch is used around the world in elementary, middle, and high schools. Computer science professors also use Scratch as a means of introducing programming concepts to college students.

HOW CAN SCRATCH BE USED TO EDUCATE IN SCHOOLS?

Schools can use Scratch to aid teachers in different subjects like mathematics, English, music, art, design, and information technology. Scratch is designed for exploration and experimentation, so it supports many different learning styles.

No matter what you use Scratch for—whether for creative storytelling, unique video games, or simple demonstrations of programming concepts—Scratch will provide a space for

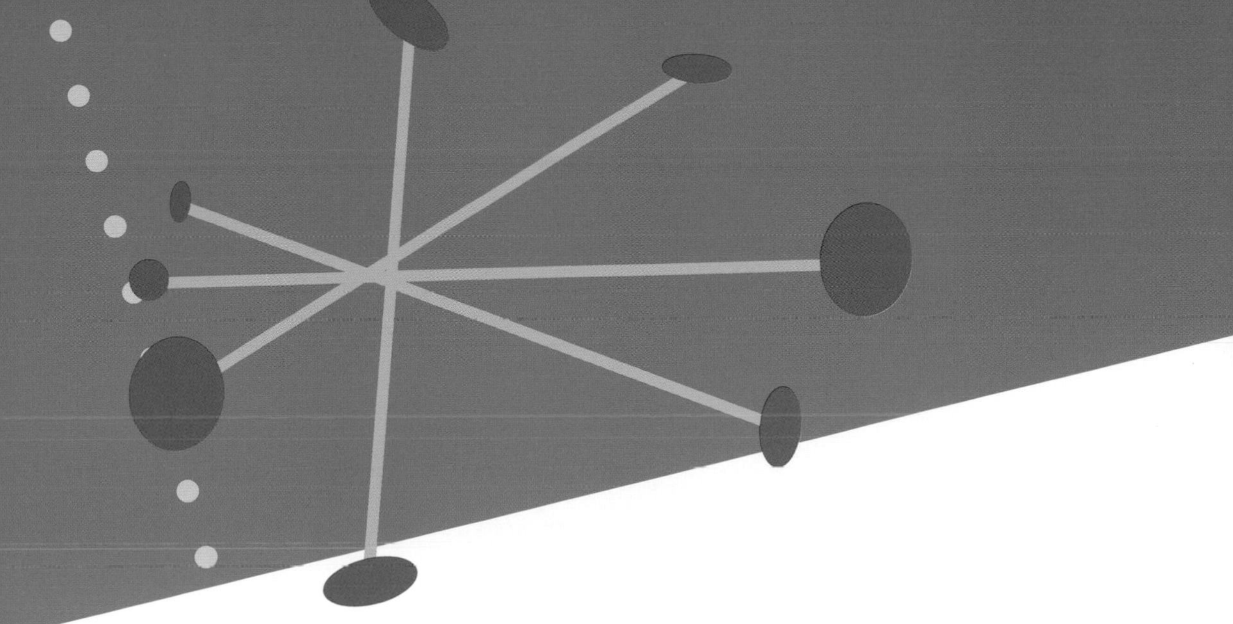

students to explore and imagine. By engaging in design-based activity individually or in groups, students will develop a greater motivation to learn.

Here are just a few of the things that students have used Scratch to do:

- A school in New York City used Scratch to build simulations of the spread of infectious diseases.
- A group of teenagers in India used Scratch to make an animated map of their village, illustrating environmental concerns where they live.
- Students at a university in Istanbul are using Scratch to examine video game culture by rapidly prototyping their own games and testing the games with the public.
- English students in a middle school in California used Scratch to build a random story generator.
- Students in an elementary school in Russia used Scratch to build their own personalized tutorials for learning about the coordinate system and trigonometry.
- High school students in Michigan used Scratch to build a physics simulator.

The possibilities are endless. It is our sincere hope that this book inspires you to create your own games, stories, and more. See "Bonus Stage 1: Make It, Share It!" on page 147 for more on how to share your work with others.

WHAT DO I NEED TO RUN SCRATCH?

It's okay if you're using an older computer! Here are the requirements suggested by MIT:

Operating System

- Windows 2000, Windows XP, Windows Vista, or Windows 7
- Mac OS X 10.4 or later
- Ubuntu Linux version 9.04 or later (see the Scratch website for other Linux options)

Display 800 × 480 or larger

Disk At least 120 megabytes of free space

NOTE *Scratch comes with a large media library and a collection of sample projects. If you have very limited disk space, you can delete the Media and Projects folders from the Scratch folder.*

Memory Most any computer should have enough memory to run Scratch. Older computers may run Scratch slowly.

Sounds You'll need speakers (or headphones) and a microphone to record and play sound effects and music.

I STILL HAVE OTHER QUESTIONS...

You can find more information on the Scratch website:

- Visit the Scratch FAQ at *http://info.scratch.mit.edu/Support/Scratch_FAQ/*.
- Visit the Support section at *http://info.scratch.mit.edu/Support/*.

"Bonus Stage 3: Online Resources" on page 156 contains other helpful links. For updates to this book, visit *http://nostarch.com/scratch/*.

MEET THE CAST

Mitch
A computer science student who loves to make cool programs, he's passionate about movies and art, too! Mitch is an all-around good guy.

The Cosmic Defenders: Gobo, Fabu, and Pele
The Cosmic Defenders are trans-dimensional space aliens who can travel through space and time. Formally deputized by the Galactic Council, the Cosmic Defender's duty is to maintain the balance of the universe.

The Dark Wizard
He is a shapeless yet powerful and vengeful spirit, whose origins are unknown. Nothing can stop his ambition of destroying the order of space and time.

Scratchy
An energetic cat living in cyber-space, Scratchy is exactly what you'd expect from a cat on the Internet. He's quite curious and impulsive.

The Dark Minions
These pesky foes are Cosmic Defenders who have fallen to the dark side. They work for the Dark Wizard now.

STAGE 1

RIDING A FLARE FROM THE SUN

STAGE 1

A SOLAR STORM RAGES ON THE SURFACE OF THE SUN....

MY NAME IS SCRATCHY. I'M FROM CYBERSPACE.

YOU'RE FROM A COMPUTER?!

THAT'S RIGHT. I FOLLOWED THAT FLASH OF LIGHT, AND HERE I AM!

HEY MITCH. UM...IS YOUR PLANET ALWAYS SO GRAY?

NO WAY! SOMETHING'S WRONG. LET'S GO CHECK IT OUT!

WHERE IS EVERYBODY?

SOMETHING TERRIBLE IS FORMING IN THE SKY!

STAGE 1

BREAKING THE SPELL!

Chapter Focus

Let's get to know Scratch! We'll also talk about *sprites* and *coordinates*.

The Game

We need to get Scratchy the cat moving again. We'll make him dance across the Stage.

To follow along with the Secret Manual, you first need to open Scratch. Once you do, you'll see Scratchy the cat on a white background. This is a new project, so the cat doesn't do anything yet.

Scratch calls Scratchy the cat—and all the other characters and objects we add to a project—a *sprite*. Soon, we'll start giving him directions to move by using the blue blocks on the left side of the screen.

The command blocks you can give a sprite are over here. Eventually, we'll stack these together to break the magic spell and get Scratchy back on his feet. These blocks here are all blue, as they're from the Motion palette.

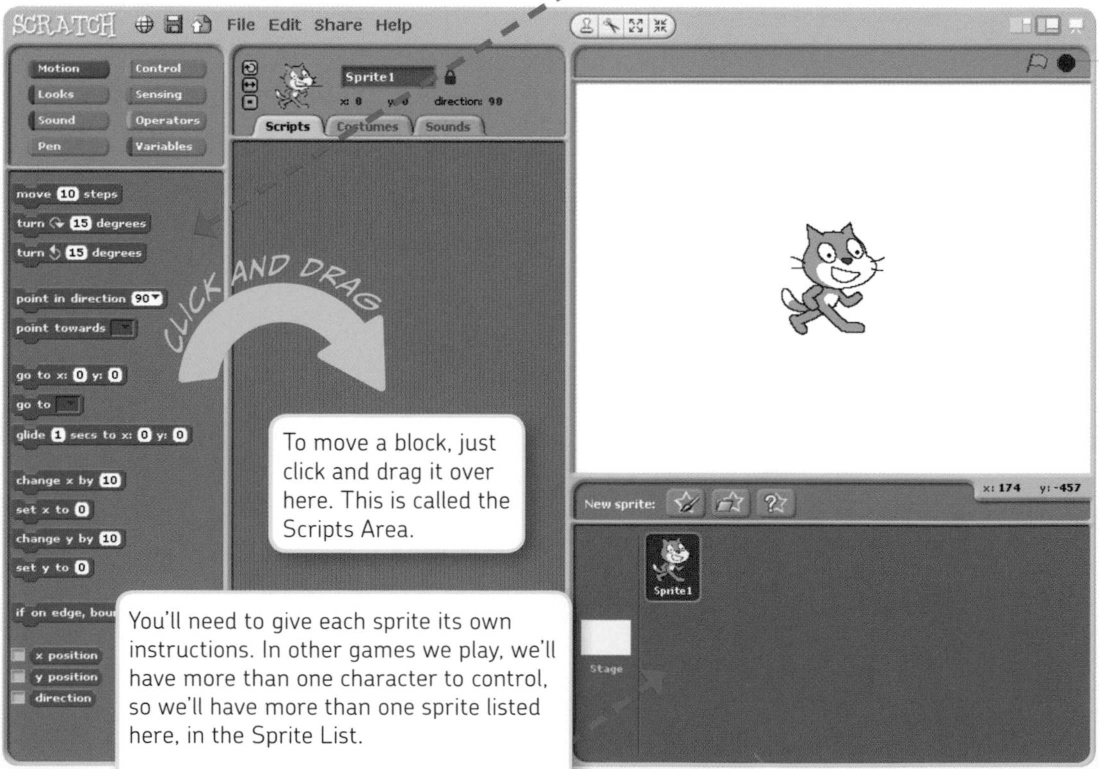

CLICK AND DRAG

To move a block, just click and drag it over here. This is called the Scripts Area.

You'll need to give each sprite its own instructions. In other games we play, we'll have more than one character to control, so we'll have more than one sprite listed here, in the Sprite List.

To give a particular sprite instructions, click a sprite in the Sprite List first and then drag blocks into the Scripts Area.

Now let's take a closer look at the rest of the interface...

A Guided Tour of the Scratch Interface!

Palette
Each of these eight buttons lets you choose functions (called *blocks*) for programming your sprites. You can combine these command blocks in stacks to create programs that control objects on the screen.

Rotation Settings
You can control how a sprite rotates in three ways:

- Can rotate freely
- Can face only left or right
- No rotating allowed

Sprite Information
This section shows the sprite's name, position, and direction it is facing (the little blue line).

Stage Settings
There are three ways to display the Stage, where your creation appears:

- Small
- Normal
- Full Screen

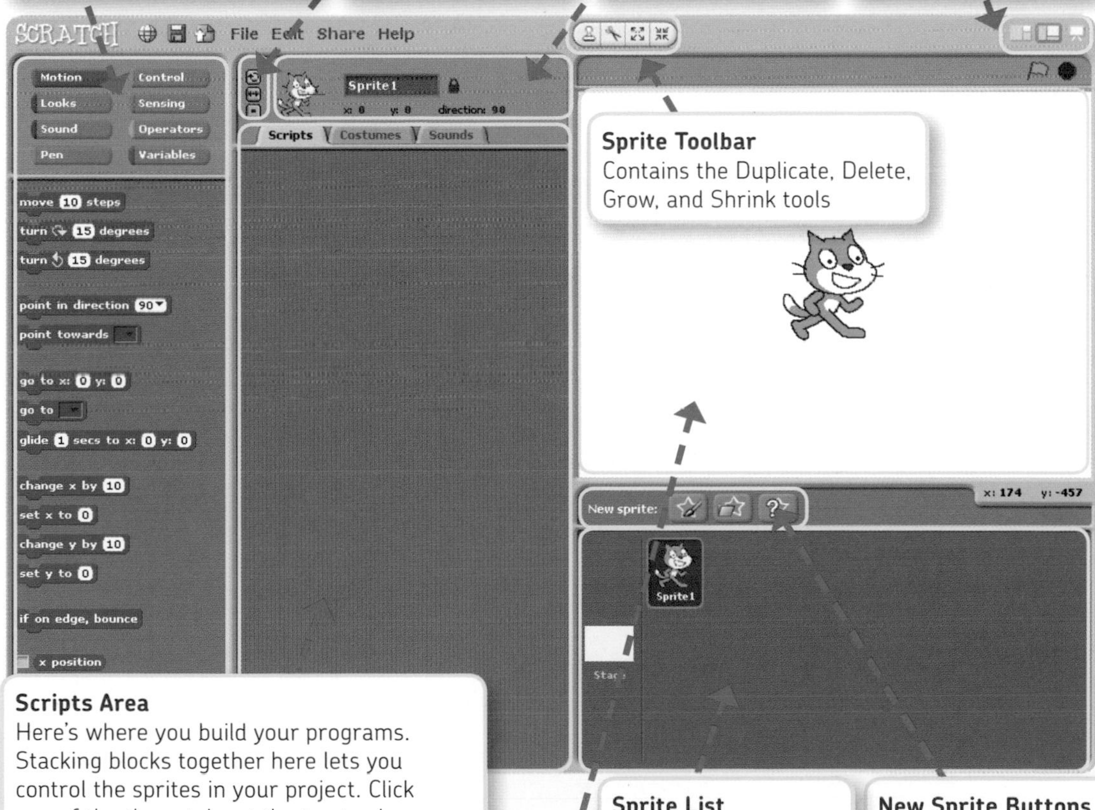

Sprite Toolbar
Contains the Duplicate, Delete, Grow, and Shrink tools

Scripts Area
Here's where you build your programs. Stacking blocks together here lets you control the sprites in your project. Click one of the three tabs at the top to change to other functions:

Scripts: Allows you to drag command blocks from the Palette and piece them together to write a program

Costumes: Allows you to draw, import, or edit images for a sprite

Sounds: Allows you to record or import sound files for a sprite to use

Sprite List
Here are the characters and objects you've created, including the Stage itself. Click the icons to edit each sprite individually.

New Sprite Buttons
There are three ways to add a sprite:

- Draw a new one
- Import an image that already exists
- Let Scratch choose one at random

Stage
Displays your creation

To use Scratch to program movements, you first have to understand how Scratch positions things.

Click the **Stage** icon in the Sprite List. Switch to the **Backgrounds** tab in the Scripts Area and choose **Import**. Note: Sprites have costumes while the Stage has backgrounds.

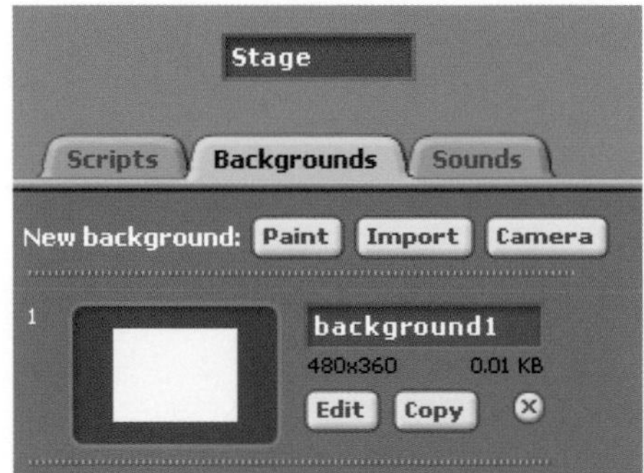

Choose the *xy-grid* background and click **OK** to import it.

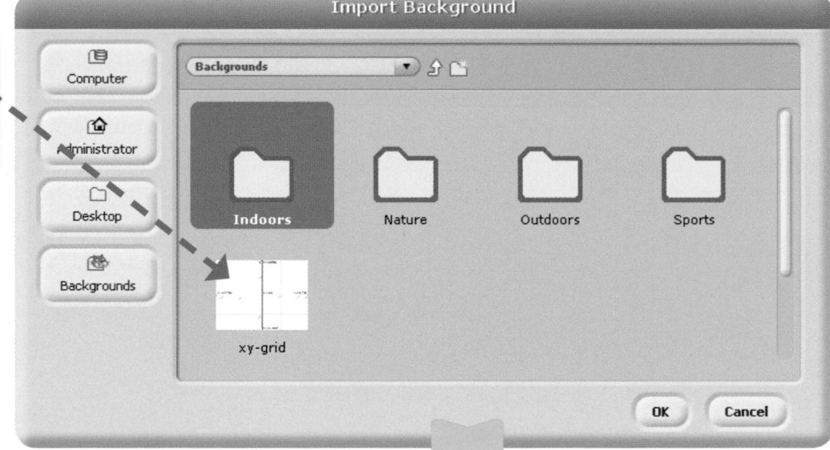

Now you can see how Scratch positions objects. Everything is on a grid with two axes:

- **y-axis:** A vertical line that marks up and down positions; ranges from -180 (lowest) to +180 (highest)
- **x-axis:** A horizontal line that marks left and right positions; ranges from -240 (farthest left) to +240 (farthest right)

Scratchy's position is at the point where the x-axis and y-axis meet. His coordinates are (X: 0, Y: 0).

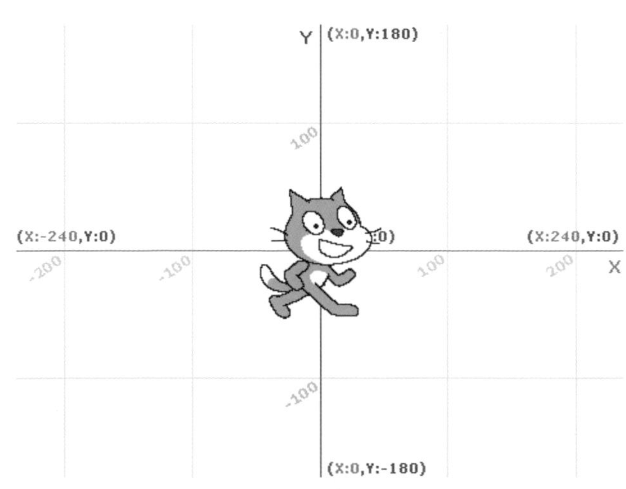

Now we can program movements for Scratchy the cat!

First, drag him to the top of the Stage, as shown on the right.

Note: The bottom-right corner displays the coordinates of your mouse. This will be really helpful when we start setting the positions of sprites!

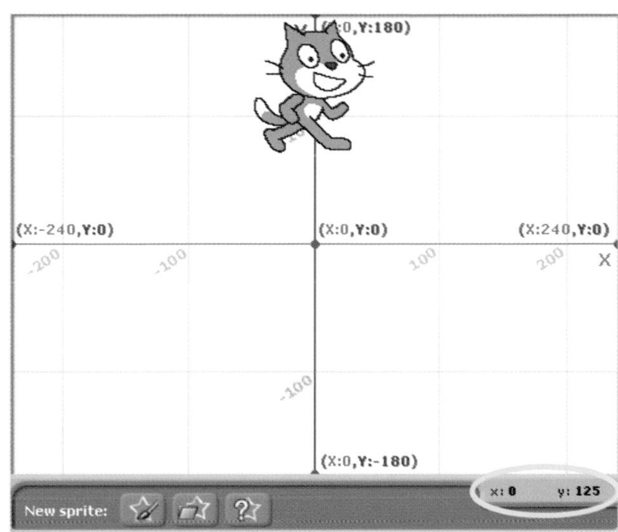

To make sure we're giving Scratchy the cat instructions, click him in the Sprite List (the box at the bottom right of the screen). Switch to the **Scripts** tab in the Scripts Area and then click the **Motion** palette (in the top left). Click and drag out the command block `go to x:0 y:0` to the Scripts Area.

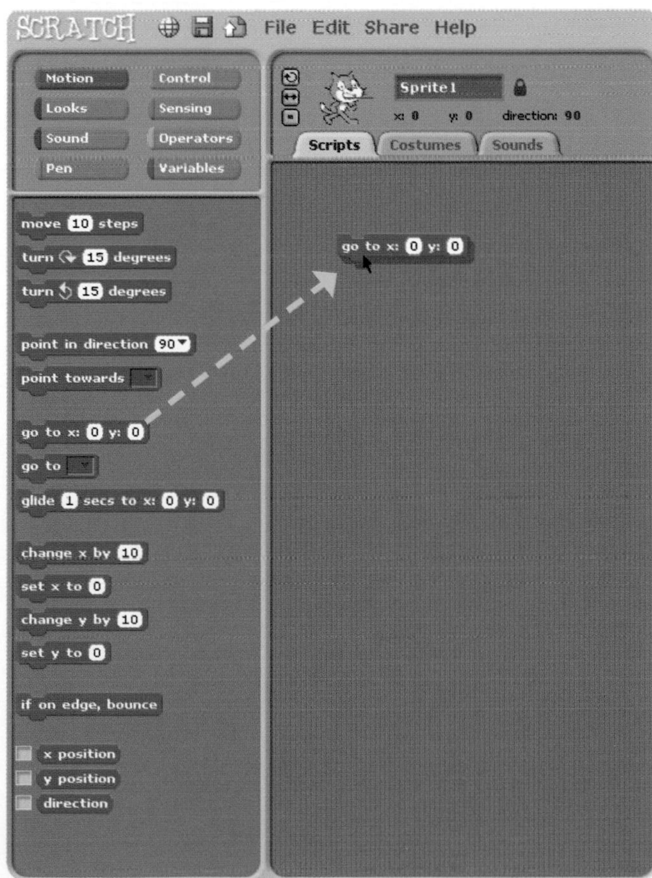

Click the number of a coordinate to change it. Set x to 0 and set y to 125. Now click the block to run it!

By doing this, no matter where we drag Scratchy on the Stage, when the program starts running, he will automatically go to this position!

We want Scratchy to move around, but at the moment, he moves too fast for us to see!

To make him move slower, click the **Control** palette and drag out the command `wait 1 secs` to the Scripts Area. Make sure to drag it under your blue command block. Wait for a white line to appear and then release the mouse.

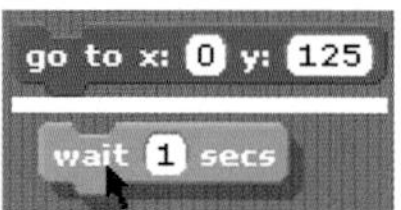

The two commands are joined together! Now change the time to 0.1 secs.

Tip: If you want to separate the commands, simply drag away the block. If you want to delete a block, simply drag it back to the Palette.

Next, select the **Duplicate** button on the Sprite Toolbar and stamp it on the commands to make five copies.

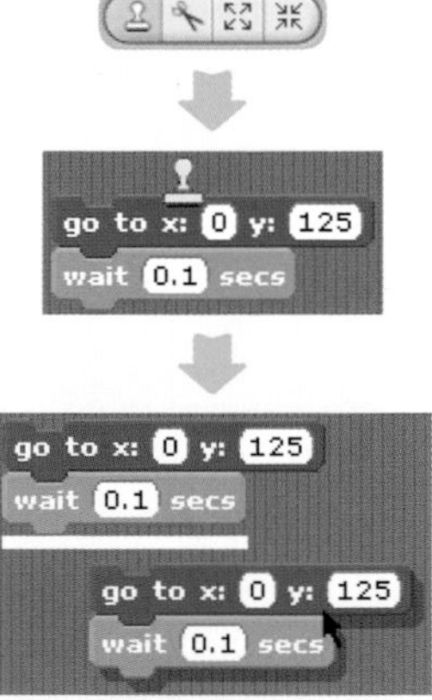

Follow this picture and type these coordinates. When you're finished, click the whole command block to make Scratchy jump around in a pentagon shape!

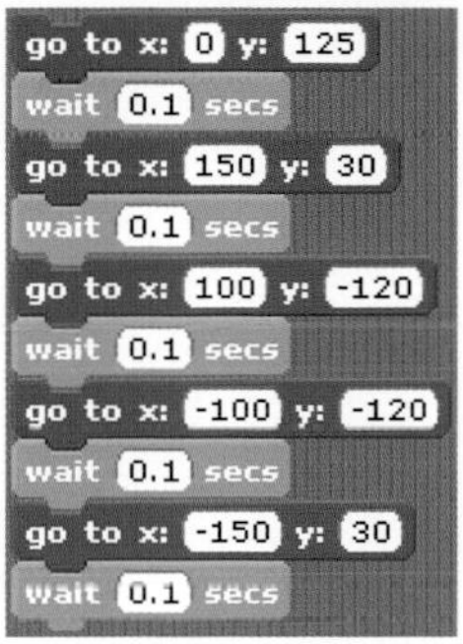

```
go to x: 0 y: 125
wait 0.1 secs
go to x: 150 y: 30
wait 0.1 secs
go to x: 100 y: -120
wait 0.1 secs
go to x: -100 y: -120
wait 0.1 secs
go to x: -150 y: 30
wait 0.1 secs
```

To make him move in a loop continuously, drag out the command block `forever` from the **Control** palette and place it at the top of the code.

Click the block, and it will actually run! Click ● to stop Scratchy from moving around. You can test any program in this way—just click it with your mouse.

Tip: Whenever you're writing scripts, you'll want to test them every now and then to see if they work the way you expect.

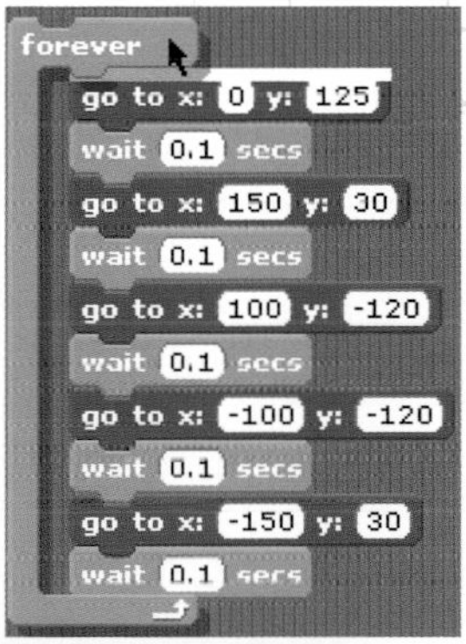

```
forever
    go to x: 0 y: 125
    wait 0.1 secs
    go to x: 150 y: 30
    wait 0.1 secs
    go to x: 100 y: -120
    wait 0.1 secs
    go to x: -100 y: -120
    wait 0.1 secs
    go to x: -150 y: 30
    wait 0.1 secs
```

Now let's make Scratchy glide around instead of jumping from point to point.

To do this, click the **Motion** palette, drag out five `glide` commands, and join them together. Follow the picture on the right, and copy the seconds and coordinates. Once you're finished, click the script to see the results!

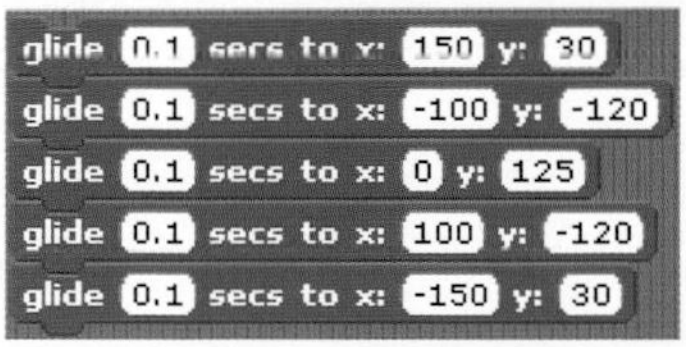

```
glide 0.1 secs to x: 150 y: 30
glide 0.1 secs to x: -100 y: -120
glide 0.1 secs to x: 0 y: 125
glide 0.1 secs to x: 100 y: -120
glide 0.1 secs to x: -150 y: 30
```

Now we can join these two programs together! From the **Control** palette, drag out the `When ⚑ clicked` command and put it at the top of your two scripts.

Tip: We'll often need multiple scripts to start at the same time, and using the `When ⚑ clicked` command will help us do that.

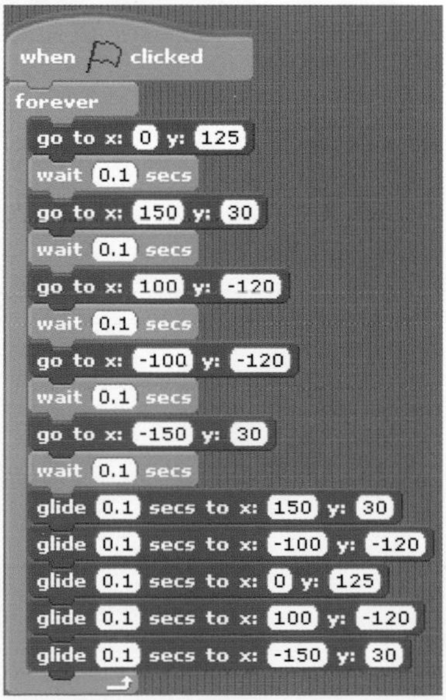

```
when ⚑ clicked
forever
    go to x: 0 y: 125
    wait 0.1 secs
    go to x: 150 y: 30
    wait 0.1 secs
    go to x: 100 y: -120
    wait 0.1 secs
    go to x: -100 y: -120
    wait 0.1 secs
    go to x: -150 y: 30
    wait 0.1 secs
    glide 0.1 secs to x: 150 y: 30
    glide 0.1 secs to x: -100 y: -120
    glide 0.1 secs to x: 0 y: 125
    glide 0.1 secs to x: 100 y: -120
    glide 0.1 secs to x: -150 y: 30
```

STAGE 1

Click these buttons above the Stage to start (⚑) and stop (●) the game.

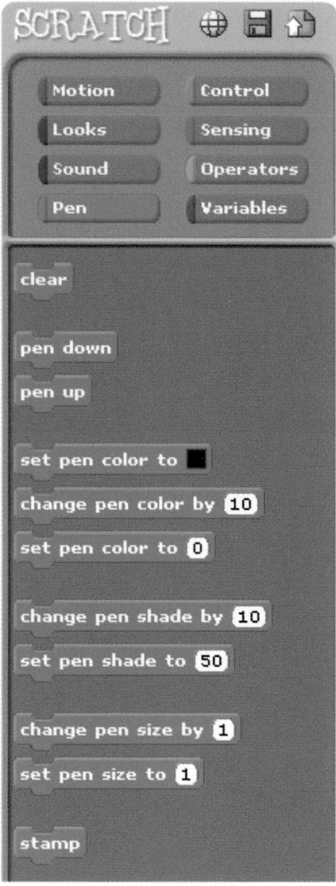

Next, click the **Pen** palette and drag out the four green Pen blocks shown on the right. Now when Scratchy moves, he'll draw the *magic star web* as well!

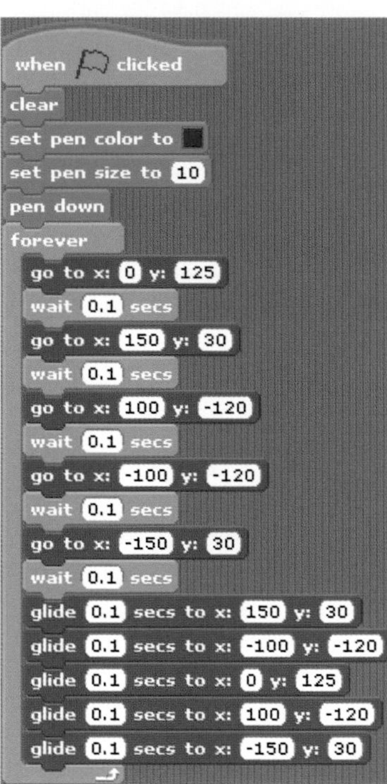

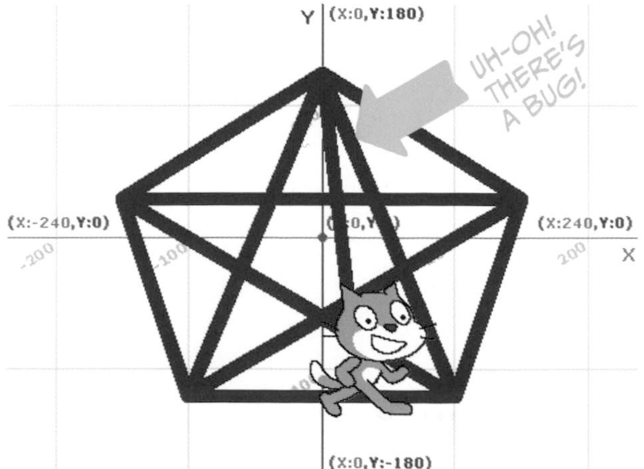

Occasionally, when you run your program, there is a *software bug*. This is the most exciting part of computer programming: discovering an error in something you have made and then solving the problem. In this case, sometimes Scratchy will draw an odd line at the beginning of the program. If we drag Scratchy anywhere else on the Stage, he draws an extra line because he starts in the wrong place. Try dragging Scratchy around and running the program multiple times by clicking ⚑ to see if you can spot the bug.

This software bug can be fixed by adding some more code—that is, new blocks—to your program. In this case, simply place a new go to block (from the blue **Motion** palette) above the green Pen blocks and below the When ⚐ clicked block.

With this little correction, Scratchy will always begin drawing from the correct position in the grid. The bug is gone!

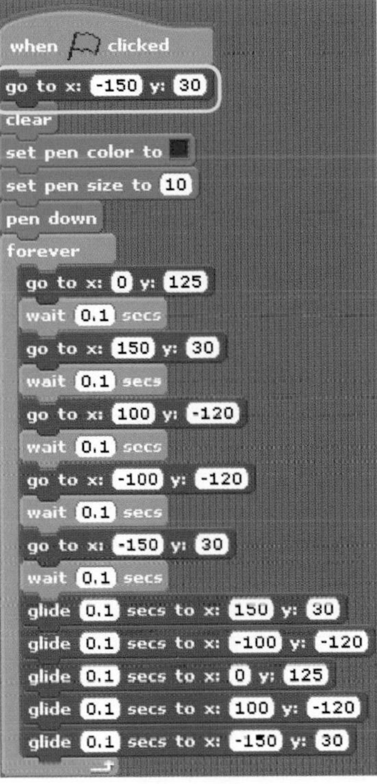

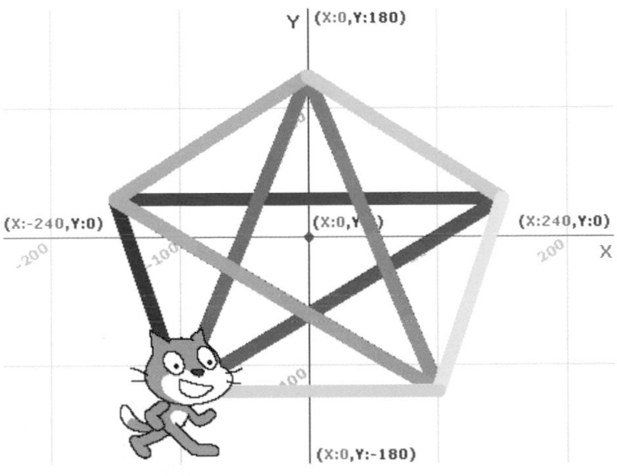

Let's add a whole new program to make a magic star web that changes colors. Build a second stack of blocks that uses the change pen color by command and see what happens.

Isn't that cool? You can give a single sprite more than one set of blocks! Scratchy now has two programs.

1 STAGE

Remember to save this file when you're finished so you can edit it later!

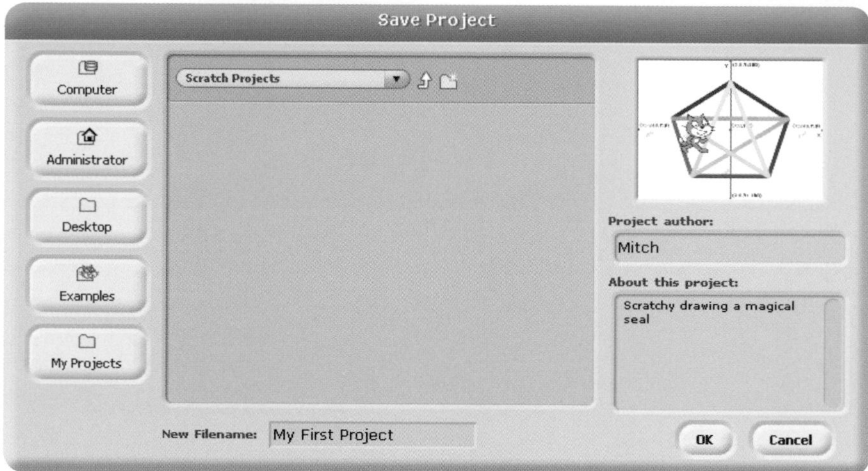

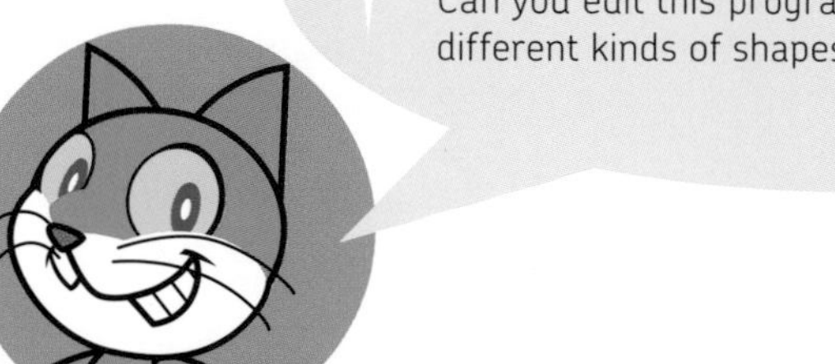

Scratchy's Challenge!!

Can you edit this program to make Scratchy draw different kinds of shapes? Give it a try!

STAGE 2

ENTERING SPACE

STAGE 2

WHO ARE YOU AGAIN?

THIS UNIVERSE IS NOW CONTROLLED BY THE DARK WIZARD AND HIS MINIONS. THEY FROZE ALL THE COSMIC DEFENDERS BESIDES ME— AND ALL THE HUMANS ON EARTH.

OH NO! WE'RE THE ONLY ONES LEFT!

THIS SECRET MANUAL SAVED US. MAYBE IT CAN HELP OTHER PEOPLE AS WELL!

YES! IF I LEARN TO PROGRAM, IT MIGHT HELP TO DEFEAT THE DARK WIZARD!

GREAT IDEA! YOU CAN DESIGN NEW EQUIPMENT AND EVEN CONTROL OUR MOVEMENTS!

OH NO! MY FELLOW DEFENDERS ARE IN TROUBLE! CHANGE INTO A SPACE SUIT AND SAVE THEM, KIND FELINE!

ALRIGHT! BUT WHY DOES SCRATCHY NEED THE SPACE SUIT?

WE NEED THE ENERGY FROM SEVEN DIMENSIONAL STRINGS TO OPEN THE STARGATE AND REACH MY FRIENDS...
...BUT INSIDE THE VORTEX, THERE'S NO OXYGEN, AND LIGHTNING CAN MAKE THINGS DISAPPEAR!

I'M READY!
BY THE WAY, GOBO, MY NAME IS SCRATCHY, AND HE'S MITCH!

WOW! IT'S FULL OF STARS!
THE ADVENTURE INTO SPACE BEGINS...

STAGE 2

A SPACE ODYSSEY!

Chapter Focus

Learn to design new costumes and program a sprite's movements, reactions, and sound effects.

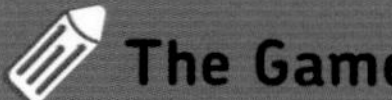

The Game

Help Scratchy avoid the lightning bolts to collect seven dimensional strings. Once all are collected, the Monolith will appear!

First, help Scratchy put on his space suit!

Click Scratchy's sprite icon, and then click the **Costumes** tab. Click the **Edit** button of the costume you want to change to open the Paint Editor.

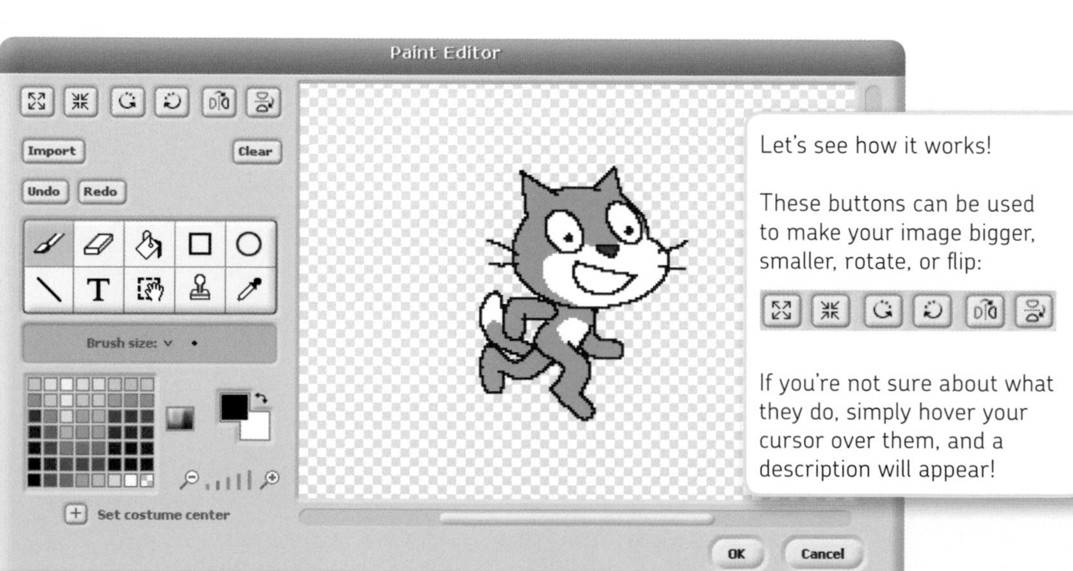

Let's see how it works!

These buttons can be used to make your image bigger, smaller, rotate, or flip:

If you're not sure about what they do, simply hover your cursor over them, and a description will appear!

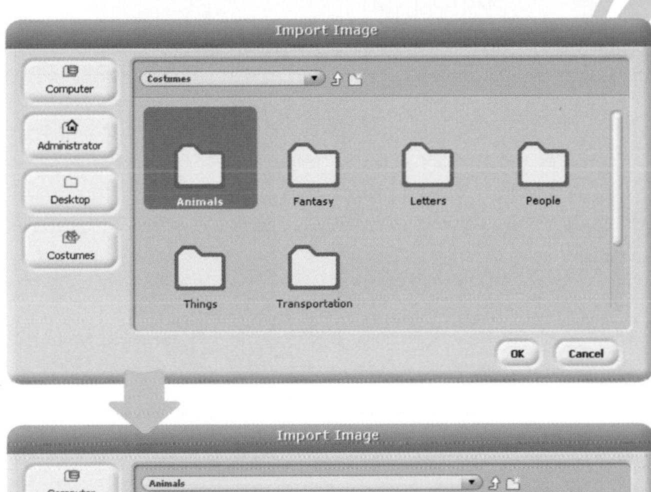

Some of the editor's buttons have names that tell you exactly what they do. Clicking **Import** shows you all of Scratch's images. This button also allows you to choose images from your own computer. Scratch supports most kinds of images.

Undo and **Redo** let you experiment with new techniques and revert them if you don't like how they look. **Clear** removes everything from the editor.

The **Paintbrush** and **Eraser** tools make it easy to draw. The size of these tools can be adjusted if you want to make a big drawing or add fine detail. Just click **Brush size** and select a new size.

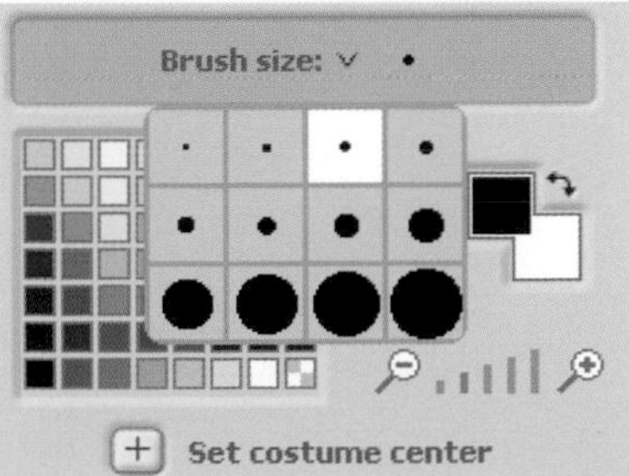

Use the **Fill** tool to color big parts of your drawing at once. You can choose a single color from the palette or use a gradient effect from the Tool Options.

Click the **Zoom** buttons (the magnifying glasses on the bottom right) to zoom in or out on your creations. This will make it easier to draw!

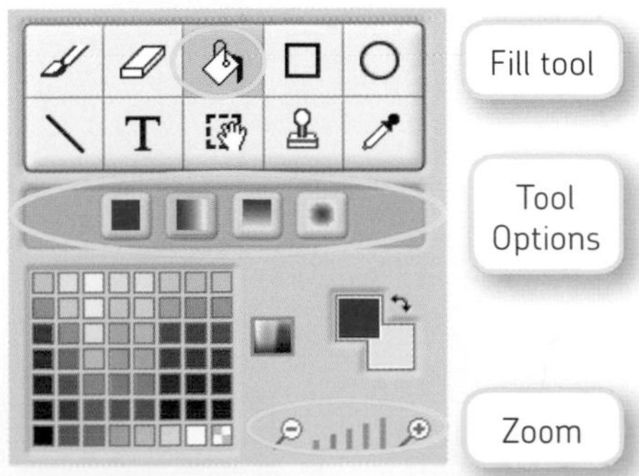

In the upper-right corner of the tool panel, you'll see tools used to draw rectangles and ellipses. These shapes can be empty inside or filled in. Try experimenting with different colors for the inside and outside. If you press the SHIFT key when you start to draw, you'll have a perfect circle or square! (You can also use this SHIFT trick when using the **Line** tool at the bottom-left corner of the panel to draw a straight line.)

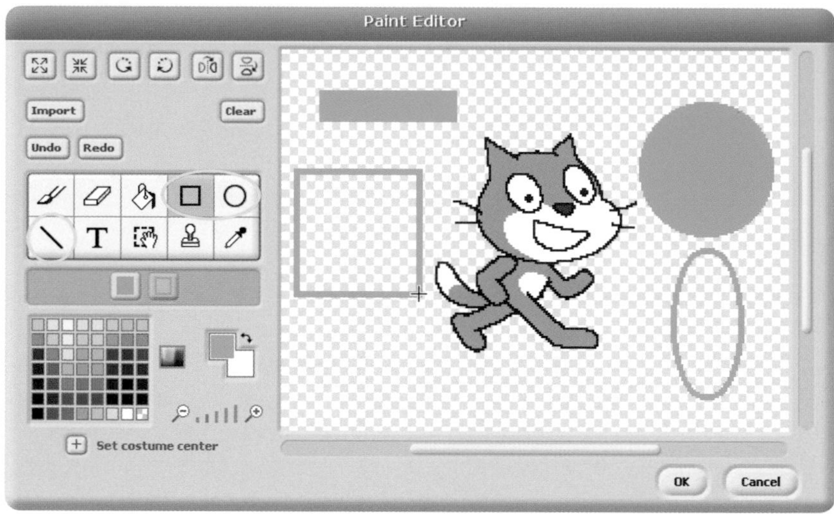

The **Text** tool lets you set the font type and size. If you want to move the text, simply click and drag the black square. Note that you can have only one text box per image.

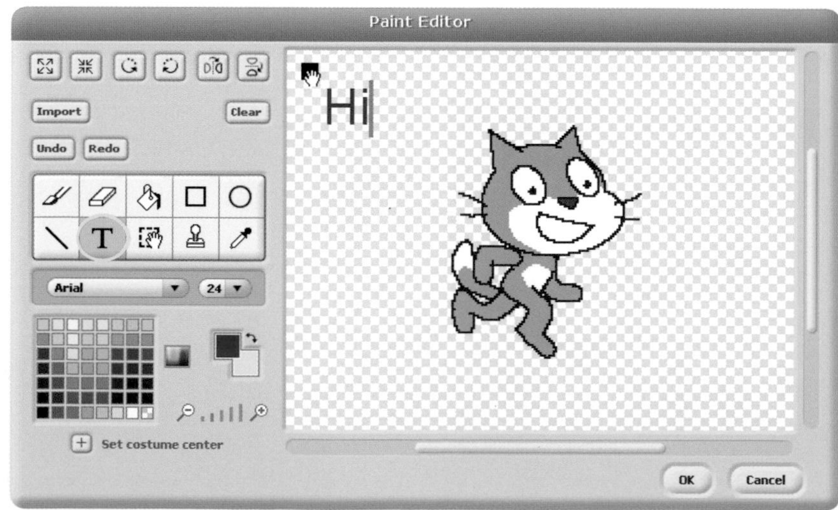

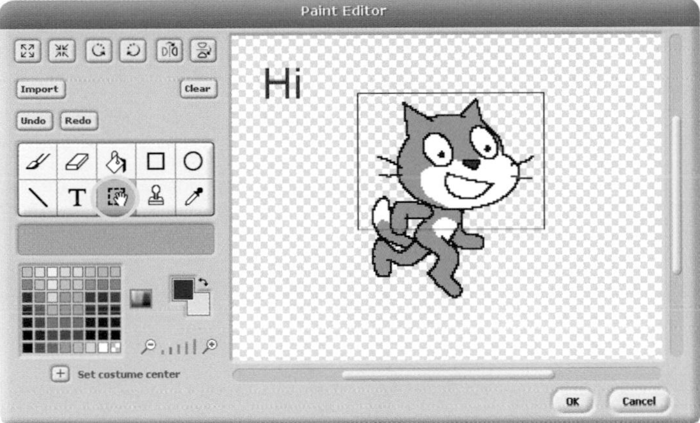

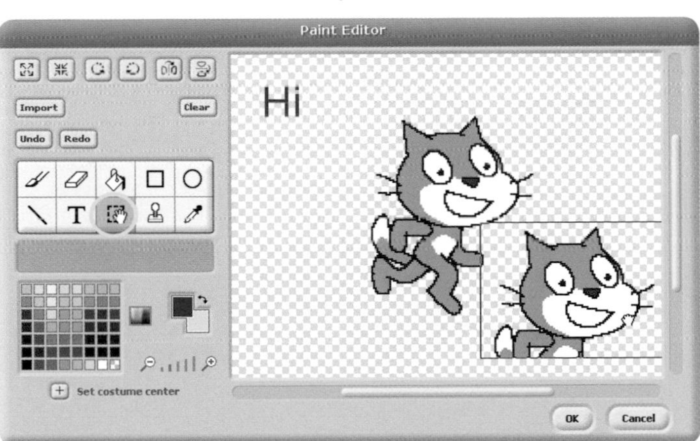

To use the **Select** tool, use your mouse to create a frame around a certain area. Then you can move, copy, or delete that area:

- Click and drag the selection to move it to a new location.
- Press and hold the CTRL key and C key at the same time to copy the image area (Mac users can use ⌘-C instead).
- Press the DELETE key to erase the selection.

The **Eyedropper** tool will match the current color to any color you click in your image.

By using the **Stamp** tool, you can copy and stamp a selected area as many times as you want! Just draw a frame around the area you want to copy and then click wherever you want to paste.

2 STAGE

Under the palette is the **Set costume center** button, which marks the center of your sprite. This helps to make sure your sprite doesn't end up in the wrong place when it spins or rotates!

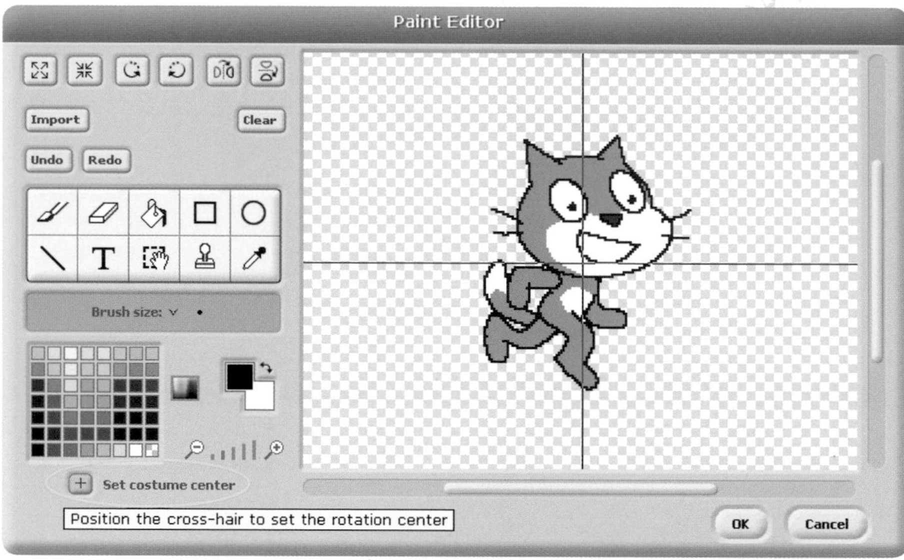

Once you know how to use the Paint Editor's tools, Scratchy can put on his space suit! Go ahead and draw your own.

If your space suit for Scratchy isn't as pretty as this one, don't worry! And if you'd like to use our sprite instead, click [icon] and you can find it in the *Super Scratch* folder as *Astro-Cat*.

Select the horizontal rotation setting (circled above) so Scratchy will face only left and right.

Now we have the main character for our game: Scratchy the astronaut!

Next, we need to add other features to our game by making more sprites. Click [paintbrush icon] to draw a new sprite.

First, let's design the String and the Monolith. They are two costumes for the same sprite, which lets us easily switch costumes during the game without having to write a program for each object. After you've finished drawing your dimensional string, click the **Paint** button in the **Costumes** tab to draw the Monolith as a second costume.

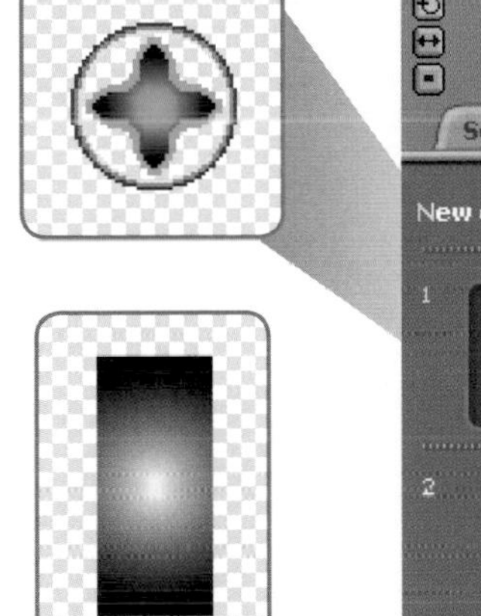

Now we'll add a third new sprite. Draw some scary lightning!

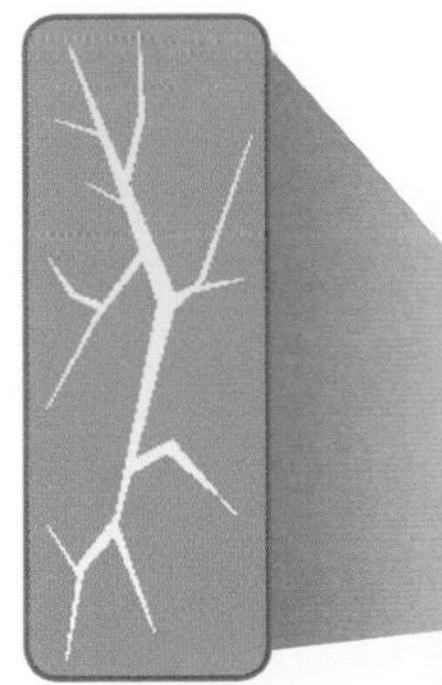

We also need to add the instructions that appear at the start of the game. We'll call this sprite Banner.

Get 7 Dimension Strings to open the Stargate!!

Avoid the Lightning or you will disappear!!

2 STAGE

Next, we'll edit the Stage so it looks like outer space. We'll use artwork of a black hole from NASA! In the **Backgrounds** tab, click the **Import** button and select *Quasar* in the *Super Scratch* folder.

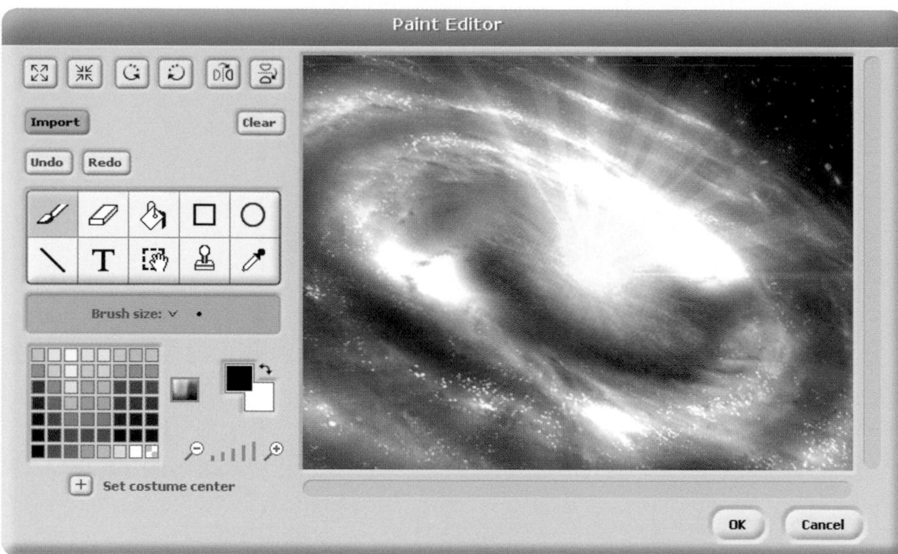

Now that we have a bunch of sprites for the game, you can see how they'll appear in the Sprite List. To give a sprite new instructions or costumes, you'll first have to click it in the Sprite List. Let's start by giving Scratchy the astronaut his programming.

Let's write our first program ❶ for Scratchy! Make sure he's selected in the Sprite List, and you've clicked the **Scripts** tab. His first program is a short one that makes him bounce up and down a little. This makes him look like he's floating in zero gravity!

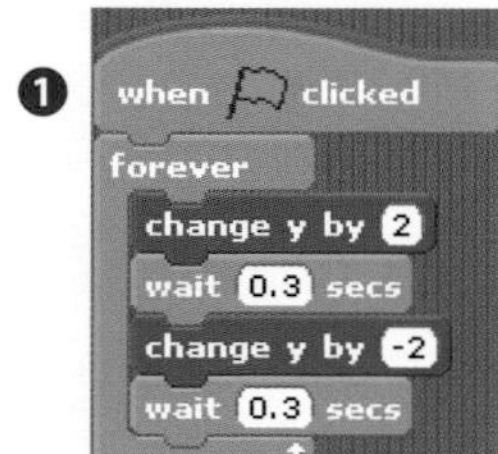

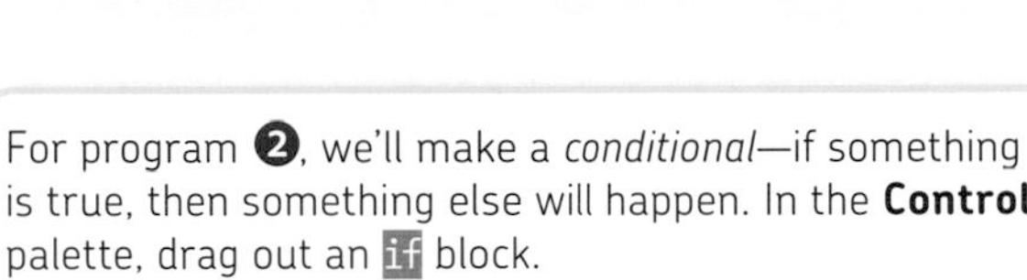

❷

```
when [flag] clicked
point in direction 90
go to x: 0 y: 0
wait 1 secs
forever
  if key up arrow pressed?
    change y by 15
  if key down arrow pressed?
    change y by -15
  if key left arrow pressed?
    point in direction -90
    change x by -15
  if key right arrow pressed?
    point in direction 90
    change x by 15
```

For program ❷, we'll make a *conditional*—if something is true, then something else will happen. In the **Control** palette, drag out an `if` block.

Then for the diamond shape, drag the **Sensing** block `key ______ pressed?`. Right below the `if`, put what you want to happen when the statement is true. Drag out the rest of these commands to form the complete program. Now you can move Scratchy up, down, left, and right by using the keyboard!

Now we'll give Scratchy two more programs. We'll need to program them individually, and then use `When [flag] clicked` to make them all run at the same time.

❸

```
when [flag] clicked
switch to costume Astro-Cat
forever
  go to front
```

❹

```
when [flag] clicked
clear graphic effects
forever if touching Lightning ?
  repeat 10
    change ghost effect by 1
```

Let's write programs ❸ and ❹. Click the **Control** and **Looks** palettes and drag out these commands.

Program ❸ controls which costume Scratchy wears, and program ❹ makes Scratchy become invisible like a ghost each time he gets struck by lightning.

When you've finished all of this, Scratchy's programming is complete!

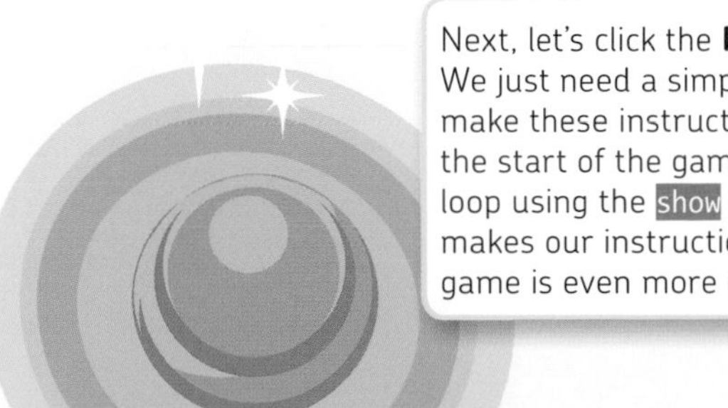

Next, let's click the **Banner** sprite. We just need a simple program to make these instructions appear at the start of the game. The `repeat 2` loop using the `show` and `hide` blocks makes our instructions flash, so the game is even more exciting.

```
when [flag] clicked
hide
go to x: 0 y: 0
go to front
repeat 2
  show
  wait 0.4 secs
  hide
  wait 0.1 secs
```

Now we can add sound effects to the game! First, click the **Stage** in the Sprite List. Then click its **Sounds** tab. You can create whatever kind of music you like for the game or even record your own voice or music.

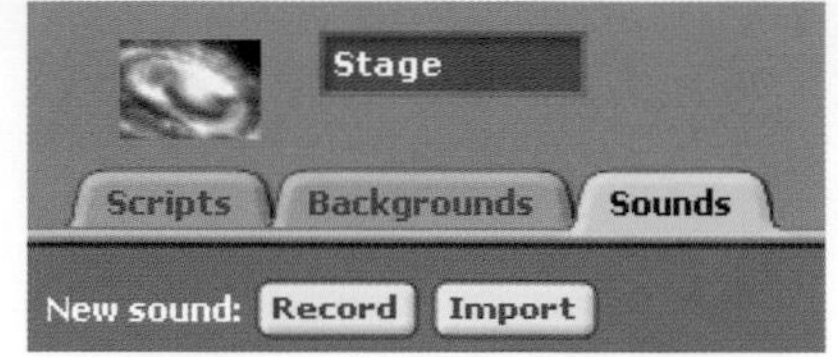

If you click the **Record** button, a sound recorder will pop up. You can click the red button to record speech or sound effects through a microphone. When you're finished, click **OK**.

Note: To record your own sounds, you'll need a microphone attached to the computer. To listen to sound effects and music, you'll need speakers.

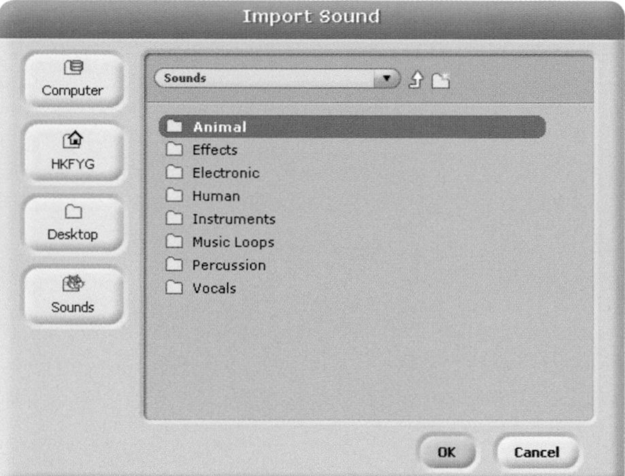

If you want to use sounds that are prerecorded, you can select **Import** to open the sound files database or choose files from your own computer (MP3 and compressed WAV, AIF, and AU formats are supported).

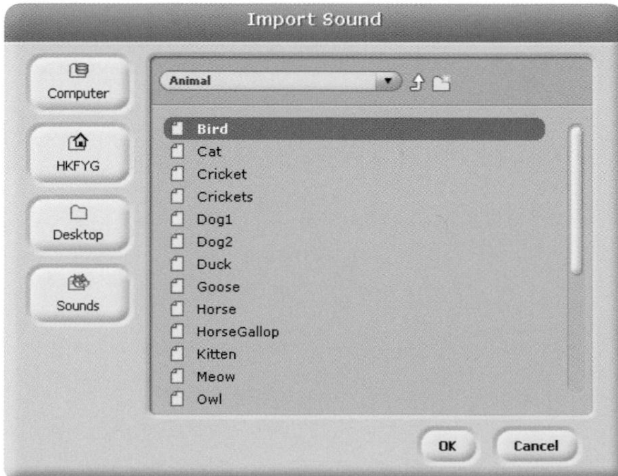

Now we can add some simple programs to the Stage. The first one makes its background change colors. In the second program, use the **Sound** palette to add a song to the Stage. Don't forget you'll need to add the music first in the **Sounds** tab.

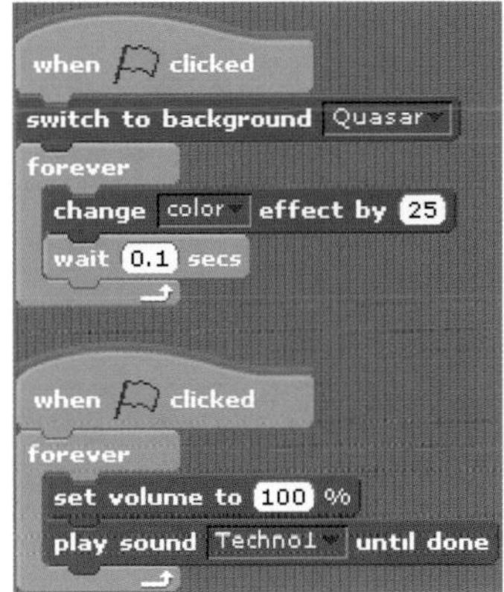

Next, we can add some sound effects to the String and Lightning sprites to make the game more exciting!

Add a new sound by pressing **Record** or **Import** in the **Sounds** tab of each sprite.

```
String
x: -100 y: 26    direction: 115
Scripts   Costumes   Sounds
New sound: Record Import
1  Humming
   0:00:01   34 KB
```

For the Lightning sprite, write a program so that whenever Scratchy touches a lightning bolt, a sound will play.

```
when clicked
wait 1 secs
forever
  if touching Astro-Cat ?
    set volume to 30 %
    play sound Thunder until done
```

Go to the **Control**, **Looks**, and **Operators** palettes and program these commands to have the lightning bolt randomly grow bigger or smaller, making the game more magical.

```
when [flag] clicked
forever
    set size to (pick random 30 to 60) %
```

Next, write this program to make the lightning disappear whenever Scratchy touches it and to control the way it moves.

The lightning's vertical position (y-axis) changes because we repeat eight times the subtraction of 40 steps (-40) from its original y-coordinate of 260. To make the lightning move differently, you can change and play with these numbers.

To create the disappearing effect of the lightning bolt, we must make sure that each time it moves—that is, the position of its y-axis changes—the program will check if it touches Scratchy.

```
when [flag] clicked
hide
wait 1 secs
forever
    wait (pick random 0 to 1.5) secs
    go to x: (pick random -210 to 210) y: 260
    go to front
    go back 1 layers
    show
    repeat 8
        change y by -40
        wait 0.3 secs
        if touching Astro-Cat ?
            hide
    hide
```

Tip: Sometimes when you're programming with the hide and show blocks while you're working on the program—running it, testing it, and checking for bugs—a sprite can disappear. Simply click the show block in the **Looks** palette to make the sprite appear again.

Now it's time to program the String. Click it in the Sprite List first! Program ❶ makes it change color, just like our Stage. Program ❷ will give it a simple animation, using the fisheye effect.

❶
```
when [flag] clicked
clear graphic effects
forever
    change color effect by 5
```

❷
```
when [flag] clicked
forever
    change fisheye effect by 30
    wait 0.1 secs
    change fisheye effect by 30
    wait 0.1 secs
    change fisheye effect by -30
    wait 0.1 secs
    change fisheye effect by -30
    wait 0.1 secs
```

Now for a big program. Let's start by dragging out the blocks you can see in ❸. These will control how the dimensional string spins and moves.

❸
```
repeat until <touching [Astro-Cat] ?>
    change y by (1)
    turn ↻ (5) degrees
    wait (0.1) secs
    change y by (-1)
    turn ↻ (5) degrees
    wait (0.1) secs
end
```

Small Stage

Tip: You may want to collapse the Stage so you have more room in the Scripts Area.

❹
```
repeat (7)
    go to x: (pick random (210) to (-210)) y: (pick random (150) to (-150))
    show
    repeat until <touching [Astro-Cat] ?>
        change y by (1)
        turn ↻ (5) degrees
        wait (0.1) secs
        change y by (-1)
        turn ↻ (5) degrees
        wait (0.1) secs
    end
    say [Got it!]
    set volume to (30) %
    play sound [Humming]
    wait (0.2) secs
    say [ ]
    hide
    wait (0.3) secs
end
```

Then add to your program so that it looks like ❹. This will make your dimensional string appear in a random place on the Stage seven different times. The `say` blocks and `play sound` blocks at the end of the program make sure the player knows he has grabbed a dimensional string.

❺

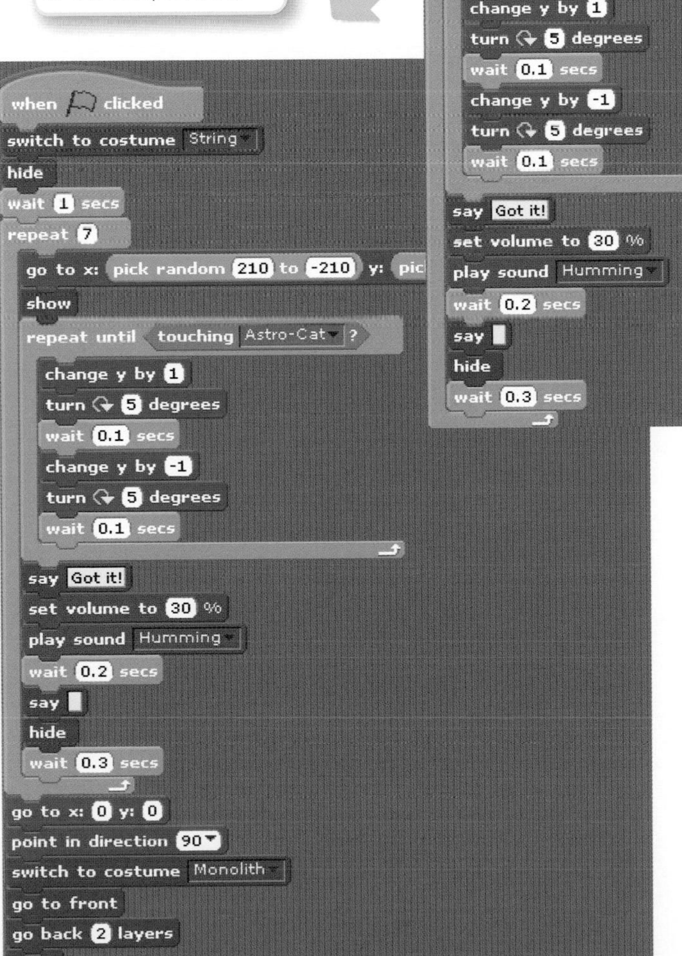

We're not done yet! This is a big script. We add a `When clicked` block at the top of our script and some instructions at the very bottom so that once Scratchy has collected seven dimensional strings, the String will change to its Monolith costume. When Scratchy touches that, he'll win the game. Make sure your finished program looks like ❺.

Now you're done! Nice work!

After saving the file, you can enjoy your final creation! Make the Stage full screen and click 🏴 to begin a new round.

Scratchy's Challenge!!

Try replacing the lightning bolt with a big, scary monster you drew yourself! Or try replacing the dimensional strings and monolith with treasure chests and a crown.

TRAPPED BY MONA LISA'S SMILE

STAGE 3

WOW, PARIS IS BEAUTIFUL!
THERE'S NO TIME TO SIGHTSEE! A COSMIC DEFENDER HAS BEEN TRAPPED IN MONA LISA'S SMILE!

HOW DEVIOUS!
THE STARGATE BROUGHT US TO PARIS...LET'S GO TO THE LOUVRE MUSEUM!

THE PAINTING'S IN THERE!
PUFF PUFF I SHOULD'VE TAKEN OFF THIS SPACE SUIT BEFORE RUNNING.

HOLD ON NOW. WE DARK MINIONS WON'T LET YOU IN SO EASILY!

RATA! BETRAYER! I CAN'T BELIEVE YOU'RE HELPING THE DARK WIZARD NOW!

ALL THE ART IN THE WORLD IS MINE NOW! *HEE HEE*

ART IS MEANT FOR SHARING. YOU CAN'T TAKE IT ALL FOR YOURSELF!

HUMPH! NOW THE PAINTING HOLDING YOUR FRIEND HAS BEEN CUT TO BITS! TAKE ON MY CHALLENGE AND THEN WE'LL TALK!

THE LOUVRE

Chapter Focus

Let's learn how to control the *flow* of a game. You'll see how to keep score using *variables* and control the order of the game using *broadcasts*.

The Game

This game is actually two games in one. First, you'll face Rata's quiz. Then you'll have to put the *Mona Lisa* back together in a puzzle game. If you get the answer wrong three times, the game ends and you lose!

First, let's import a picture of the Louvre Museum as a background to the Stage.

Photo Credit: Raphael Frey

Then we'll add a program that makes the Stage play music. The `forever` block is a special kind of command we call a *loop*. Any sound effect or music you add here keeps playing again and again, so make sure you like how it sounds!

Now we'll add a new sprite (☆) for Rata. He's called *fantasy4* in Scratch's *Fantasy* folder.

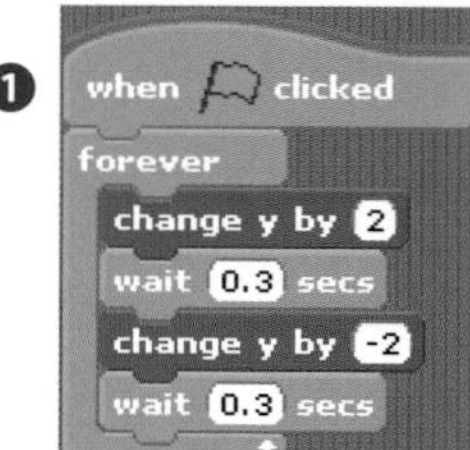

Write program ❶ first. This forever loop makes Rata float up and down.

For program ❷, go to the **Sensing** and **Looks** palettes, and use the ask and say blocks. This program asks the first question of Rata's quiz. We've made it a multiple-choice question, so the answer must be *A* or *B*.

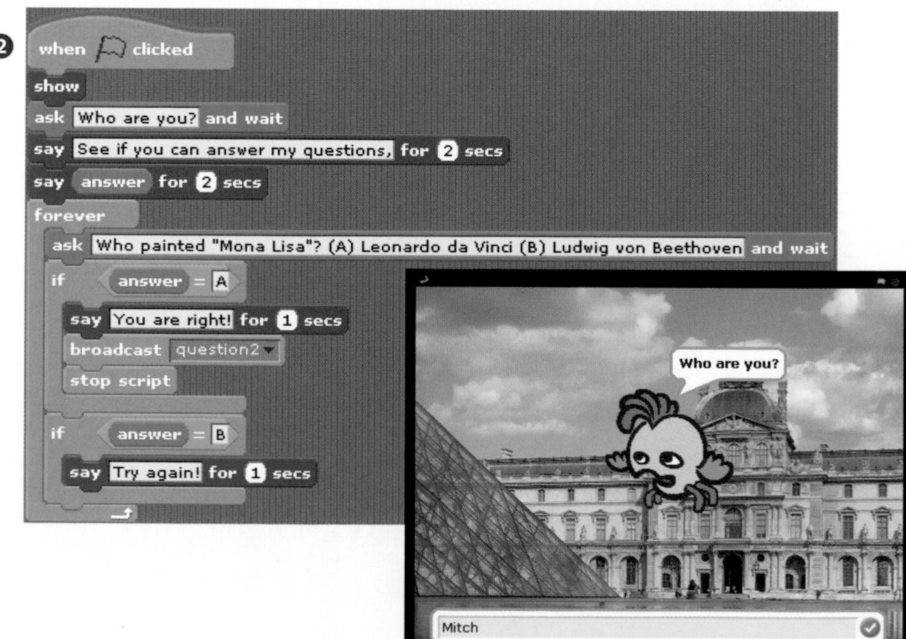

If you noticed back in program ❷, there's a command that says `broadcast question2` if you get the right answer. *Broadcasts* are like big announcements to all the programs in your project. They're a great way to connect related parts of a game. So let's try writing two more questions as new programs ❸ and ❹. These two programs wait for broadcasts `question2` and `question3` to start using the `when I receive` block.

❸
```
when I receive [question2]
forever
  ask [Where was it painted? (A) Madrid, Spain (B) Florence, Italy] and wait
  if <(answer) = [A]>
    say [Try again!] for (1) secs
  if <(answer) = [B]>
    say [You are right!] for (1) secs
    broadcast [question3]
    stop script
```

❹
```
when I receive [question3]
forever
  ask [Where is it now? (A) The Louvre, Paris (B) The Colosseum, Rome] and wait
  if <(answer) = [A]>
    say [You are right!] for (1) secs
    say [Now try to solve this puzzle!] for (2) secs
    hide
    broadcast [puzzle]
    stop script
  if <(answer) = [B]>
    say [Try again!] for (1) secs
```

When the player answers all three questions correctly, the `puzzle` broadcast signal in program ❹ tells the game that the quiz is over and the puzzle half of our game should now begin.

Import the sprite *Puzzle* from the *Super Scratch* folder (). This isn't just a single image—it's a sprite with a bunch of different costumes. The sprite's costumes include the instructions for the puzzle game and the puzzle itself. The final two costumes in this sprite display the winning screen and the message that appears when you lose.

Let's take a closer look. First, we'll display the first instruction costume.

Memorize the picture sequence!

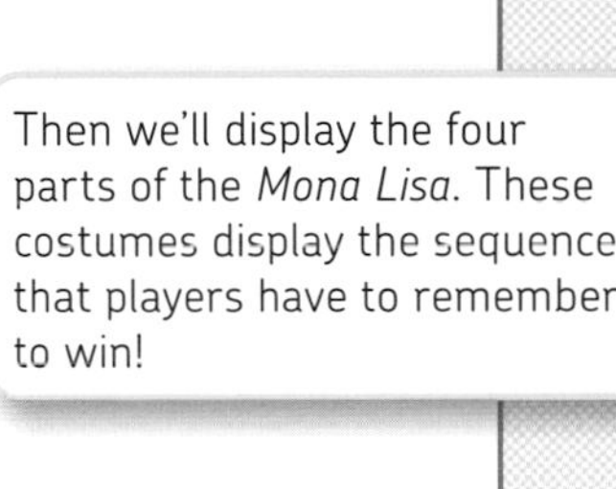

Then we'll display the four parts of the *Mona Lisa*. These costumes display the sequence that players have to remember to win!

The next three costumes display the game instructions and a start screen.

Repeat the sequence correctly!

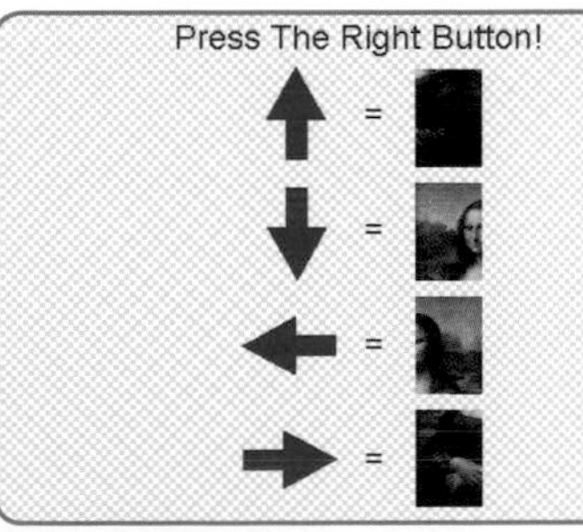

Start Now!!

Finally, we have two costumes for the winning and losing screens.

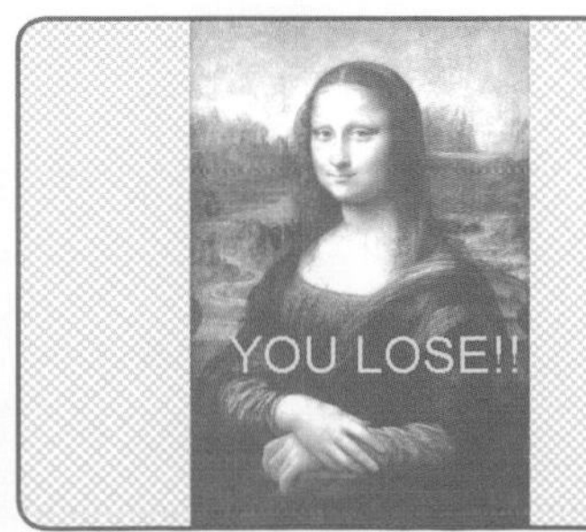

For this big sprite, we'll need a lot of programs. Let's start by adding a special kind of command called a *variable*. Variables are good for keeping track of numbers that change during a game, like scores, player health, player lives, and more.

Click **Make a variable** in the **Variables** palette, and call it Chance. The new Chance variable is how the computer knows how many times the player gets another chance to solve the puzzle before losing.

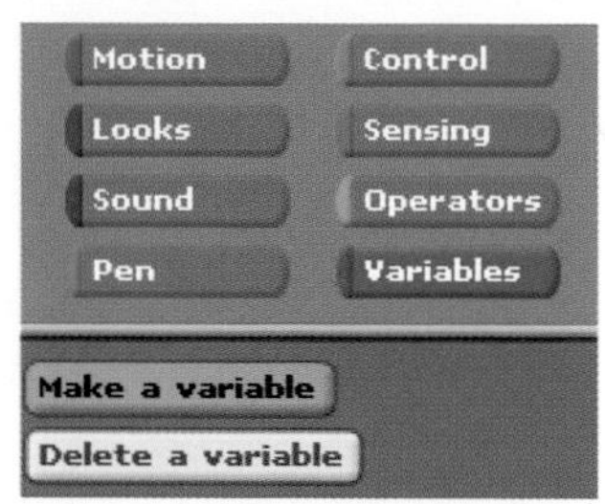

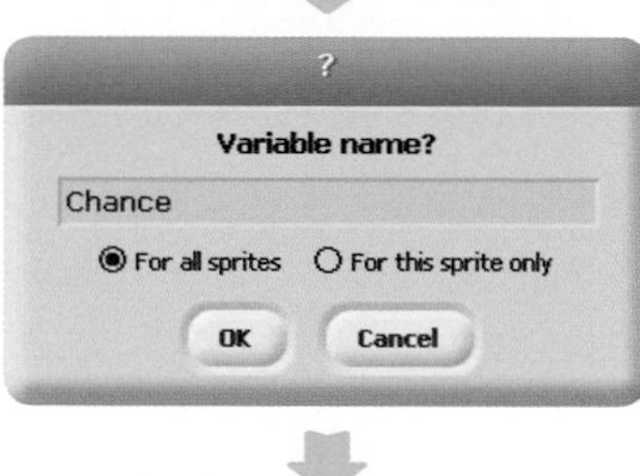

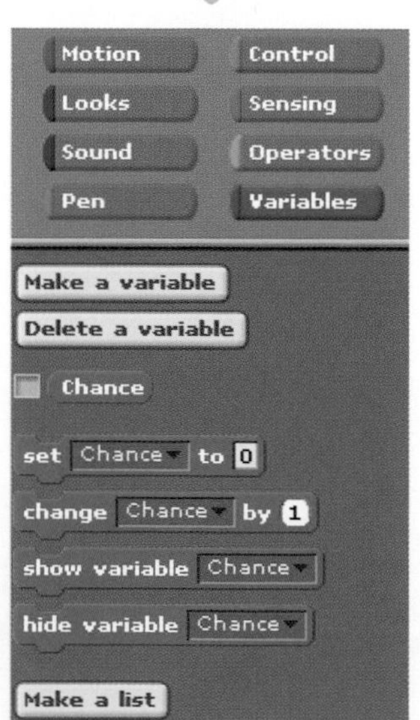

Now for the programs themselves. Add scripts ❶ and ❷. Script ❶ just hides our variable Chance during the quiz part of the game. Next, script ❷ determines how the Puzzle sprite should change costumes—just as described on pages 48–49.

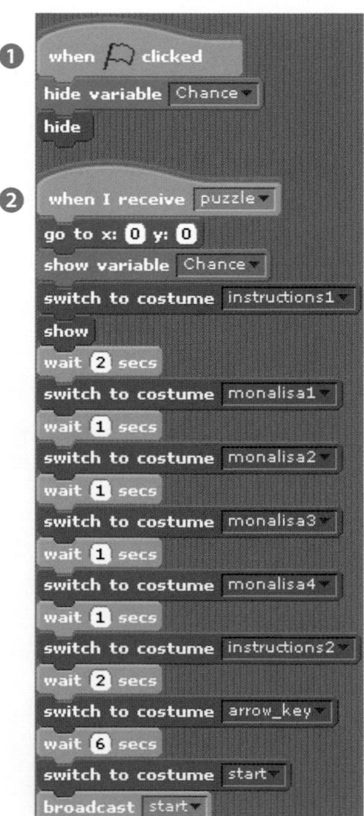

Then we'll add four different scripts: one for each right answer to the puzzle. If the player presses the wrong arrow, the sprite changes its costume and a broadcast called `wrong` is broadcast. We'll use this broadcast to control the `Chance` variable.

❸
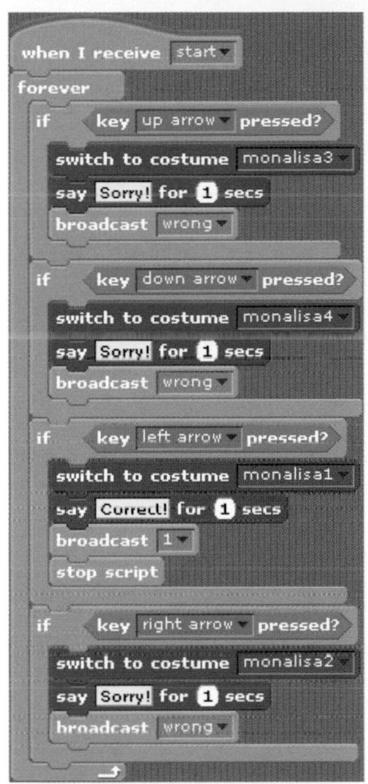

❹

❺
```
when I receive 2
forever
  if key up arrow pressed?
    switch to costume monalisa3
    say Correct! for 1 secs
    broadcast 3
    stop script
  if key down arrow pressed?
    switch to costume monalisa4
    say Sorry! for 1 secs
    broadcast wrong
  if key left arrow pressed?
    switch to costume monalisa1
    say Sorry! for 1 secs
    broadcast wrong
  if key right arrow pressed?
    switch to costume monalisa2
    say Sorry! for 1 secs
    broadcast wrong
```

❻
```
when I receive 3
forever
  if key up arrow pressed?
    switch to costume monalisa3
    say Sorry! for 1 secs
    broadcast wrong
  if key down arrow pressed?
    switch to costume monalisa4
    say Correct! for 1 secs
    broadcast win
    stop script
  if key left arrow pressed?
    switch to costume monalisa1
    say Sorry! for 1 secs
    broadcast wrong
  if key right arrow pressed?
    switch to costume monalisa2
    say Sorry! for 1 secs
    broadcast wrong
```

Notice how the broadcast named `1` at the end of script ❸ starts script ❹. Likewise, script ❺ starts only `when I receive` `3`, which is broadcast by script ❹ when the player presses the correct arrow. With all of the correct arrows pressed in script ❻, we signal a new broadcast called `win`.

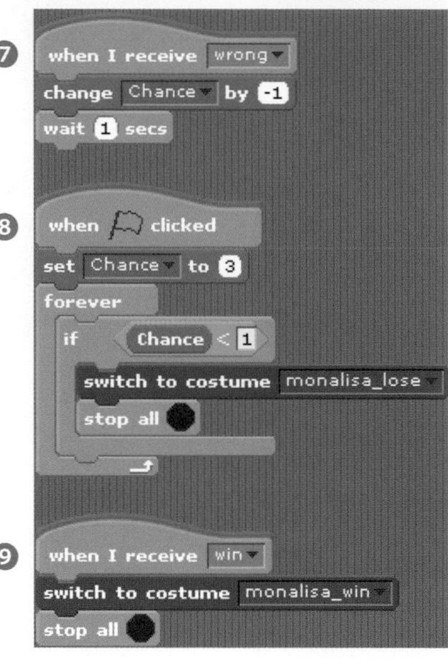

Finally, add three more programs to the Puzzle. Program ❼ subtracts 1 from the Chance variable any time it receives the wrong broadcast. Programs ❽ and ❾ control when the winning and losing screens appear.

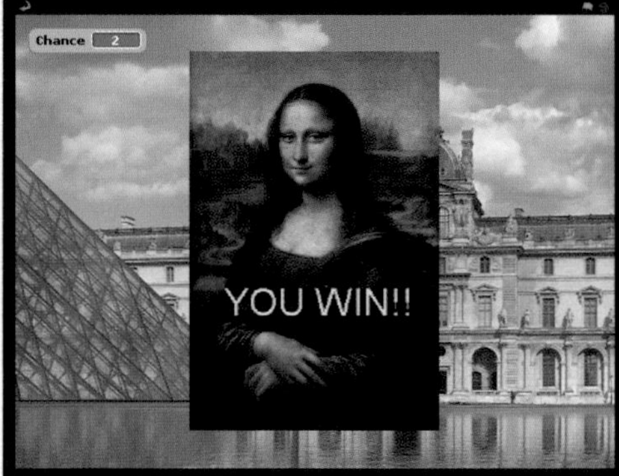

That's it! Remember to save your project (**File > Save**) before giving the game a try. Let's see if you can win this!

Scratchy's Challenge!!

Can you use the ask block and broadcasts to create a personality test? How about a flash-card game to learn words in a new language? Give it a try!

DEFEND HONG KONG'S TECHNOCORE

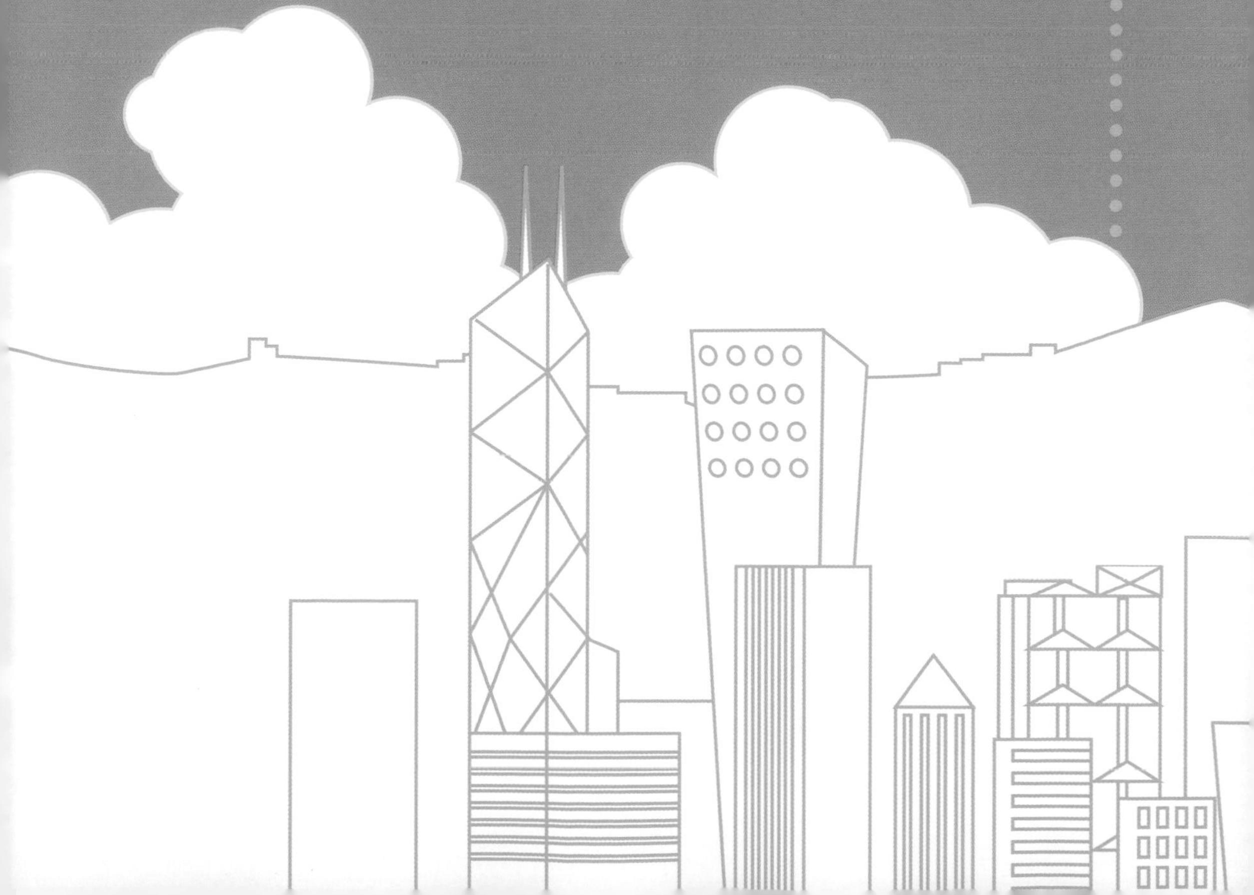

STAGE
4

MISSION COMPLETED!

FABU'S FREE AGAIN!

SNIFF FOILED AGAIN...

AWW...DON'T BE UPSET! I JUST THINK THAT ART'S MEANT TO BE SHARED!

DO YOU THINK THE COSMIC DEFENDERS WOULD TAKE ME BACK... OR JUST FORGIVE ME... IF I APOLOGIZED?

PROBABLY! BUT BE CAREFUL NOW. NEWS HAS IT THAT THE DARK WIZARD IS PLANNING TO LAUNCH A VIRUS ATTACK ON HONG KONG!

OH NO! BUT IF THAT HAPPENS, THE WHOLE DIGITAL WORLD COULD BE DESTROYED!

FABU'S RIGHT! WE HAVE TO DESTROY THE VIRUS RIGHT AWAY!

HONG KONG
HERE IT COMES!

STAND BACK. I KNOW KUNG FU!

HACK ATTACK

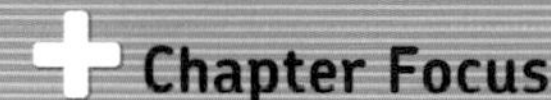

Chapter Focus

Learn to control sprites with the mouse, program objects to bounce back, and start a game by pressing the spacebar.

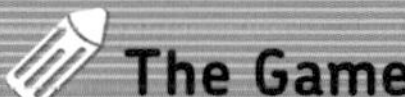

The Game

Help Scratchy attack flying viruses and stop them from touching the server at the bottom of the screen. If you successfully block 30 viruses, you win the game!

First, go to the **Stage** and import a sparkly nighttime picture of Hong Kong!

Did you know you can add programs to the Stage, too? We can add this program to make our city glow!

```
when I receive start
clear graphic effects
forever
    repeat 2
        wait 0.3 secs
        change brightness effect by -5
    repeat 2
        wait 0.3 secs
        change brightness effect by 5
```

STAGE 4

We can then add a new sprite called Instructions, which tells the player how the game works. We'll write two programs for the sprite.

Protect Hong Kong!
Defend the server from virus attacks

Click your mouse to move Scratchy!
Press <SPACE> to start!

❶
```
when [flag] clicked
go to x: 0 y: 0
show
forever
    if key space pressed?
        broadcast space
        hide
```

❷
```
when I receive space
broadcast start
```

Program ❶ makes the sprite show up at the start of the game and disappear when the player presses space, the spacebar on their keyboard.

Program ❷ makes the Instructions sprite broadcast start when it receives the space broadcast from program ❶. This will start the game!

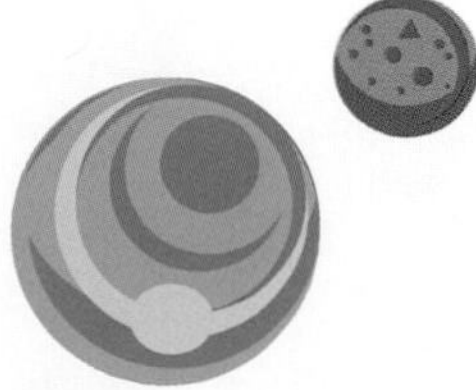

Then we'll write some programs for Scratchy. Import the sprite *Neo-Cat* from the *Super Scratch* folder into your project. Notice how he already has two costumes: one where he's just standing and another where he's jumping.

So let's add some programs to control how Scratchy looks. In program ❶, we hide him before the start broadcast is received. In program ❷, we control how Scratchy switches costumes. Whenever the player's mouse is clicked—that is, whenever mouse down?—Scratchy looks like he's jumping.

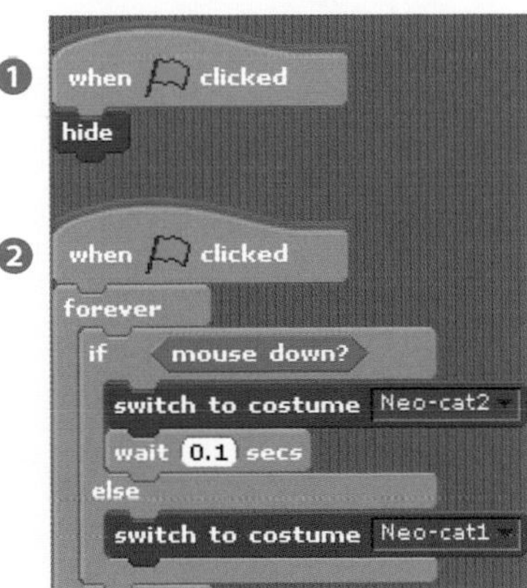

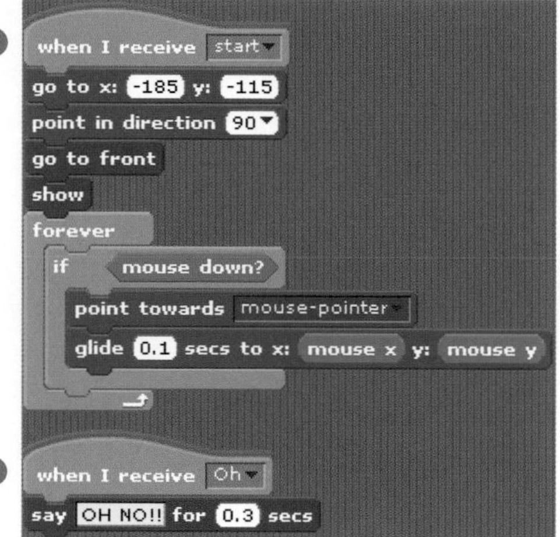

But how does the player control Scratchy? Program ❸ lets you control Scratchy with the mouse, showing him only when the start broadcast is received.

Program ❹ makes a speech bubble saying "OH NO!!" appear whenever the Scratchy sprite receives the Oh signal. We'll broadcast Oh whenever a virus manages to hit the server.

Tip: By using the mouse instead of the keyboard, the player has a lot of control over Scratchy, who will move very quickly for this game. But remember—every game is different! Sometimes the keyboard works well, too.

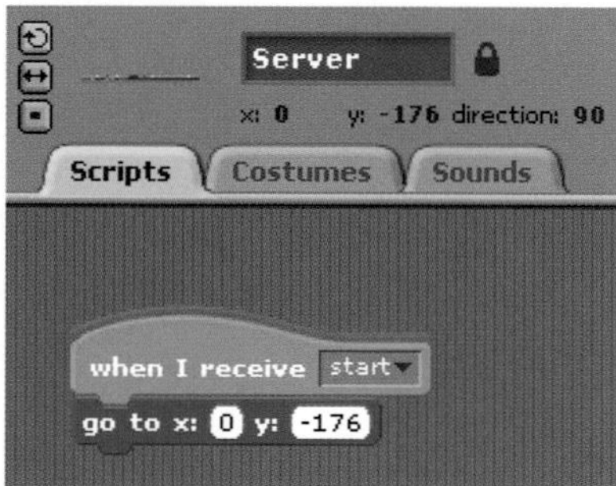

Then we'll draw or import a new sprite called Server. The Server has one simple program so that it appears in the right place: centered and at the bottom of the screen.

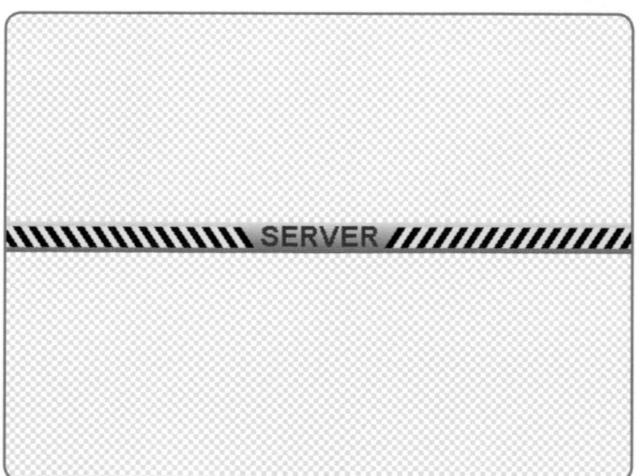

Next, import a new sprite called *Virus* from the *Super Scratch* folder. It has a set of costumes of letters spelling V-I-R-U-S.

Program ❶ hides the Virus until the game starts. Program ❷ makes the Virus switch costumes as it flies around.

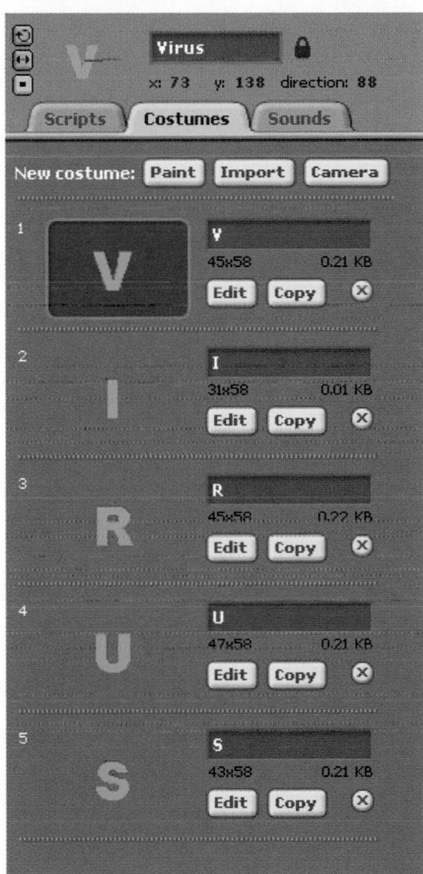

❶
❷

Program ❸ for the Virus makes it fly around. It bounces whenever it bumps into Scratchy or the edges of the screen.

❸
```
when I receive start
go to x: 0 y: 165
point towards Neo-cat
forever
    if touching Neo-cat ?
        point in direction pick random 45 to -45
    move 10 steps
    if on edge, bounce
```

Now we'll add more programs to the Virus to keep score. These programs use blocks from the **Control** and **Variables** palettes to record and signal the conditions for winning and losing.

Program ❹ creates a new variable called score and the conditions we need to meet for the script to broadcast win. Your score will now appear on the Stage.

❹

Program ❺ creates a variable called chance, which keeps track of how many times the Virus is allowed to touch the Server sprite before the player loses. We'll give Scratchy five chances to start. When you're out of chances, the program broadcasts lose. Just like the player's score, the number of tries the player has left is displayed on the Stage as chance.

❺

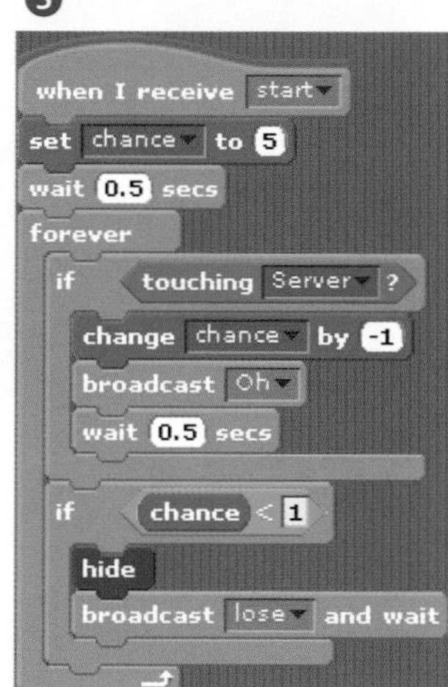

Tip: When setting the rules for winning and losing in your games, use the greater-than symbol (>) or the less-than symbol (<) instead of the equal sign (=) , as we do in programs ❹ and ❺. This will prevent the game from breaking when a variable changes too quickly!

Why might the variable change too fast in this game? Scratchy might touch the Virus a few times in quick succession, and the program won't realize that you've won the game.

Now let's add a sprite for the winning screen. Programs ❶ and ❷ keep it hidden. Then program ❸ makes it appear when the win broadcast is received from the Virus sprite.

You Win!!
The city server is safe now!

The losing screen is pretty similar to the winning screen. To save time, we can select the **Duplicate** tool and click the winning screen to copy both the image and the programming!

All we need to do now is change the costume and the last program a bit.

You Lose!!
Press <SPACE> to try again!

STAGE 4

We're finished! After you save the file, hurry and help Scratchy the hacker defend the network from the virus attack!

Scratchy's Challenge!!

How would you make this game harder for the player? How about adding different kinds of viruses? What about turning this game into a two-player Ping-Pong match? Give it a try!

PENALTY KICK IN IPANEMA

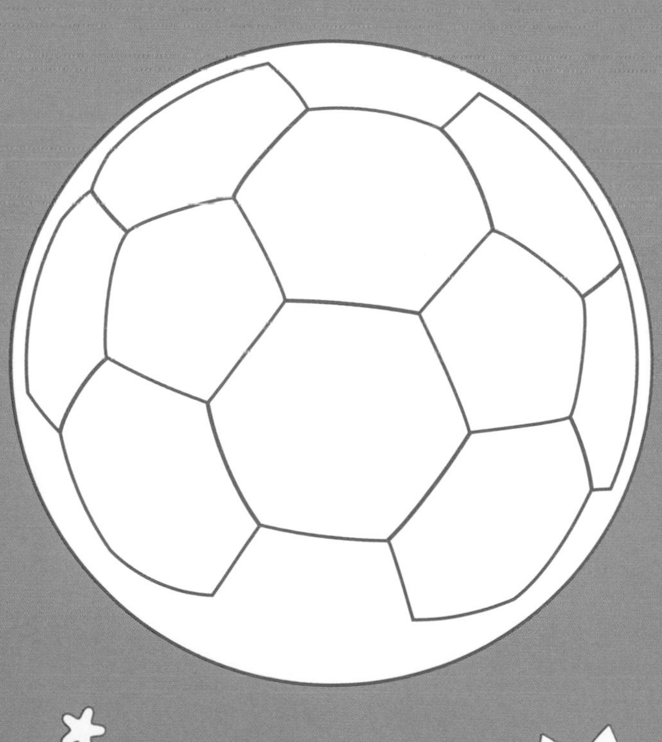

STAGE 5

ACCORDING TO THE SECRET MANUAL, THE VIRUS CAME FROM IPANEMA!

THAT'S THE FAMOUS IPANEMA BEACH IN RIO DE JANEIRO, BRAZIL!

EEK! DO I HAVE TO WEAR A SWIMSUIT?

RIO DE JANEIRO

I CAN FEEL A COSMIC DEFENDER NEARBY!

WOW...BUT EVERYONE'S FROZEN!

NOT EVERYONE... I CAN HEAR A SQUEAKING NOISE FROM FAR AWAY!

GOBO! FABU! I'M TRAPPED IN THIS GOALPOST!

HANG IN THERE, PELE... WHAT ARE WE GOING TO DO?

RIO SHOOT-OUT

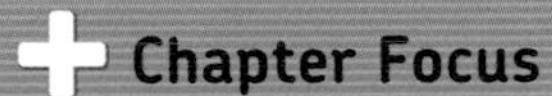

Chapter Focus

Learn how to program a soccer game with a targeting system, several related rules, interactive sound effects, and a vivid, animated background!

The Game

Shoot penalty kicks and avoid the moving goalie. You'll win the game if you manage to score five out of eight tries!

Here's a look at the final game. We'll need to create a targeting system that will move over the goal. When you press the spacebar, you'll kick the ball where the bull's-eye is. But watch out—the goalkeeper will dive every time you kick the ball!

To start, let's draw or import a background of Rio de Janeiro.

All the sprites we need for this game are in the *Super Scratch* folder. You can also import the blank file *Rio-Shootout*, which has all our sprites but no programming yet.

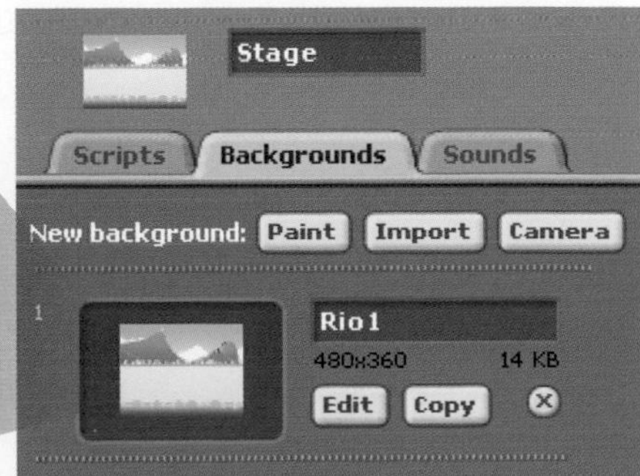

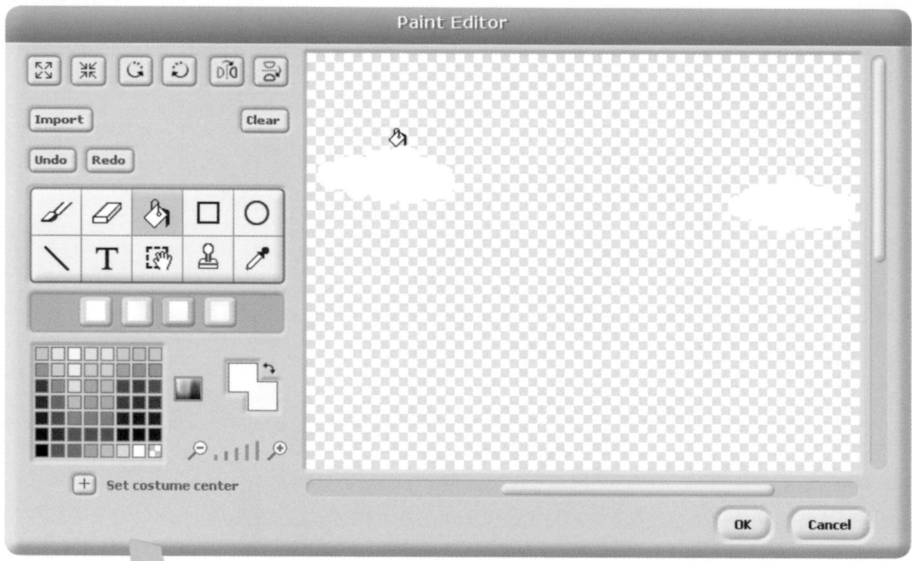

Create a sprite for the clouds, and program it to float up and down. This will make the background livelier!

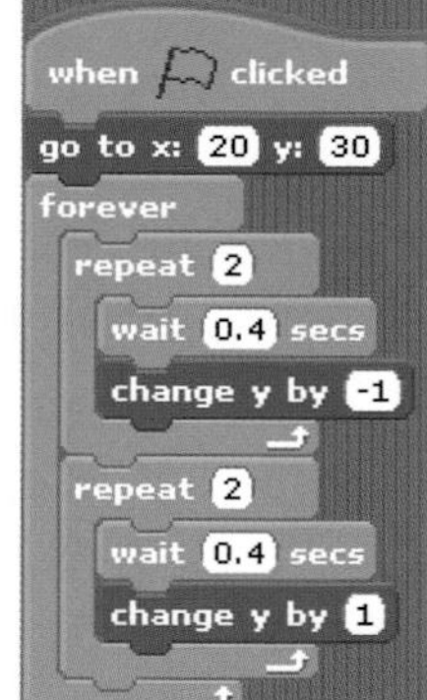

If there's a beach, there must be some waves! So we'll add a Wave sprite, too.

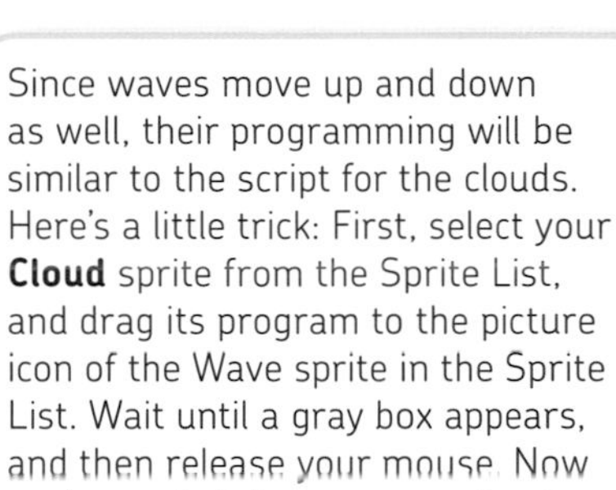

Since waves move up and down as well, their programming will be similar to the script for the clouds. Here's a little trick: First, select your **Cloud** sprite from the Sprite List, and drag its program to the picture icon of the Wave sprite in the Sprite List. Wait until a gray box appears, and then release your mouse. Now you've copied the programming for the Cloud sprite to the Wave sprite!

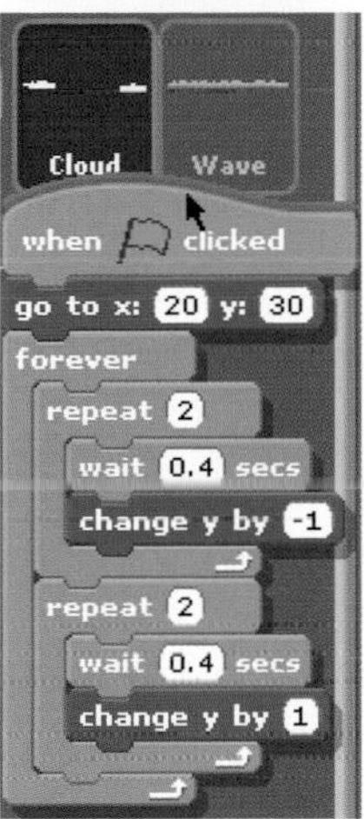

We can also change the Wave's script to make it move faster and more frequently than our clouds.

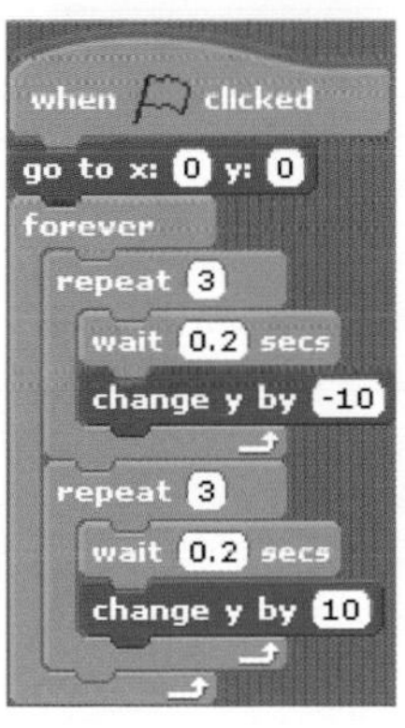

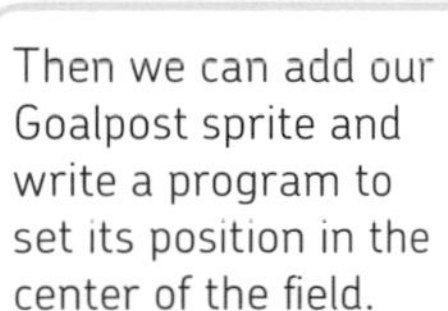

Then we can add our Goalpost sprite and write a program to set its position in the center of the field.

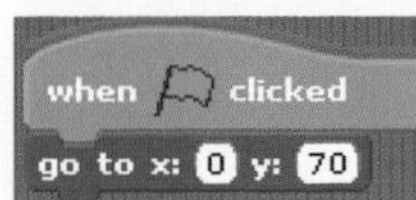

The goal's net has its own sprite. Add it to the project, and then create this short program to set its position.

Now is a good time to test your program to make sure everything appears where you want it to. Try clicking 🏴. If your clouds float, the waves lap against the beach, and your goal and net are in the right place, let's move on to programming the game itself.

Add this bull's-eye, which shows where Mitch will kick the ball.

❶ 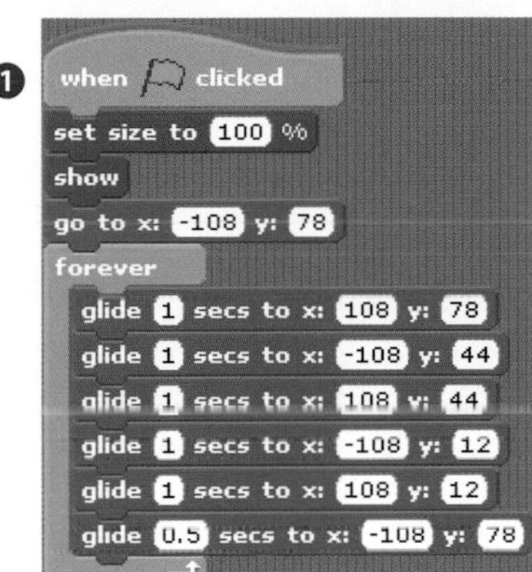

Program ❶ will make the bull's-eye zigzag across the goal.

❷ 

For program ❷, add these two set commands from the **Variables** palette in a forever loop. We'll use these variables to determine where the ball goes after Mitch kicks it. You'll need to create X and Y in the **Variables** palette.

Tip: Since our player doesn't need this information, we can hide the variables from being displayed on the screen by deselecting them in the **Variables** palette.

❸ ❹ 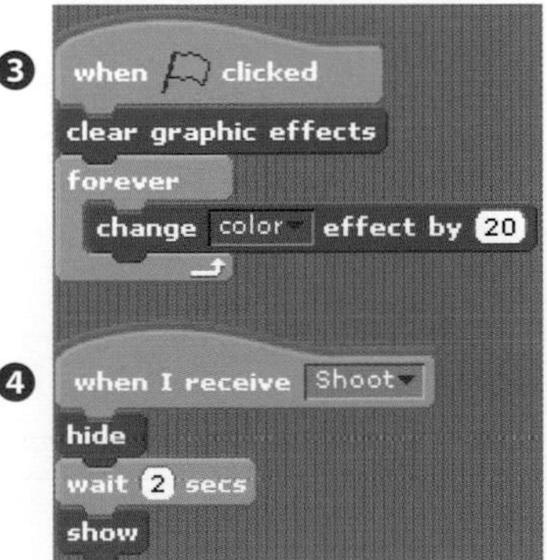

Then add in programs ❸ and ❹ to the Bullseye sprite. Program ❸ makes the bull's-eye continuously change color. Program ❹ makes the bull's-eye disappear when it receives the shoot broadcast. Now when Mitch kicks the ball, the bull's-eye will disappear.

To make this game even more fun, we gave Pele the Keeper two costumes. That means we can program a simple animation by switching costumes.

We'll write two programs for Pele. Program ❶ sets his size, costume, and starting position and then animates him using the `next costume` command in a `forever` loop.

When he receives the `Shoot` broadcast in program ❷, he'll "dive" to a random spot in the goal to try to stop the ball! The `pick random` blocks are in the **Operators** palette—just drag two right into the `glide` block.

❶
```
when [flag] clicked
set size to 45 %
switch to costume Keeper1
go to x: 0 y: 20
forever
    wait 0.5 secs
    next costume
```

❷
```
when I receive Shoot
glide 0.5 secs to x: pick random -90 to 90 y: pick random 20 to 70
wait 2 secs
go to x: 0 y: 20
```

Now we'll move on to program the game's most important feature—the ball.

First, create a Ball sprite. Then add some sound effects in the **Sounds** tab.

Next, write program ❶ to set its starting position and size, and then play the `Whistle` sound.

Tip: The first two blocks (`go to front` and `go back 1 layers`) adjust the layer value so the Ball will appear in front of the Net, Stage, and other sprites in the game.

❶
```
when [flag] clicked
go to front
go back 1 layers
set size to 50 %
go to x: 0 y: -80
play sound Whistle until done
```

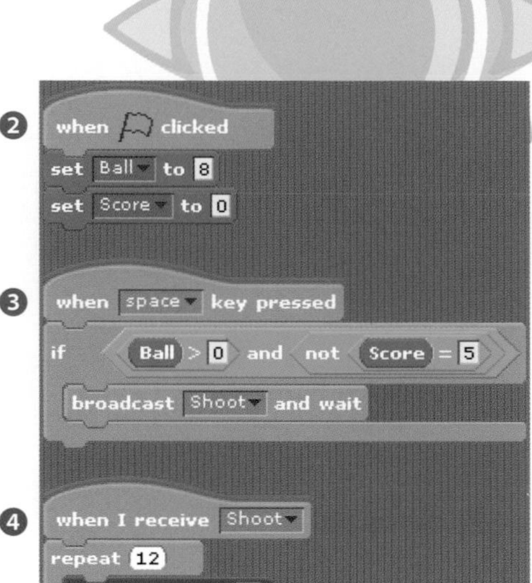

By creating variables for Ball and Score, you can keep track of how many times the player has kicked the ball and how many times he has scored a point. Program ❷ sets the starting values for these variables.

Program ❸ will broadcast Shoot whenever the spacebar is pressed. Notice how there's an if loop that uses a not block from the **Operators** palette to make sure the player isn't out of balls (Ball > 0) and hasn't won the game (Score = 5).

Program ❹ is a neat animation trick. It makes the ball shrink into the distance by using a negative value (-2) in the change size by block.

❷
```
when [flag] clicked
set Ball to 8
set Score to 0
```

❸
```
when space key pressed
if <<(Ball) > 0> and <not <(Score) = 5>>>
  broadcast Shoot and wait
```

❹
```
when I receive Shoot
repeat 12
  change size by -2
```

Program ❺ is quite special. First, it makes the ball glide to our variables X and Y. (Just drag them from the **Variables** palette right into the glide block.) The two if loops contain the game's program for scoring. It broadcasts either Goal or Miss, depending on whether or not the ball touches Pele.

❺
```
when I receive Shoot
change Ball by -1
glide 0.5 secs to x: (X) y: (Y)
if <<touching Net ?> and <not <touching Keeper ?>>>
  broadcast Goal and wait
if <<touching Net ?> and <touching Keeper ?>>
  broadcast Miss and wait
```

You'll score a goal if you manage to sneak the ball by our goalkeeper Pele!

```
6
when I receive [Goal]
change [Score] by (1)
say [GOAL!!] for (1) secs
wait (1) secs
set size to (50) %
go to x: (0) y: (-80)

7
when I receive [Miss]
change [Score] by (0)
say [Miss!!] for (1) secs
wait (1) secs
set size to (50) %
go to x: (0) y: (-80)
```

Now let's add some more programs to the Ball. In programs ❻ and ❼, we'll determine what happens after a Goal or Miss. Program ❻ will change the Score by 1, while program ❼ will change it by 0. Whether the player scores or not, the ball returns to its original position after 1 second.

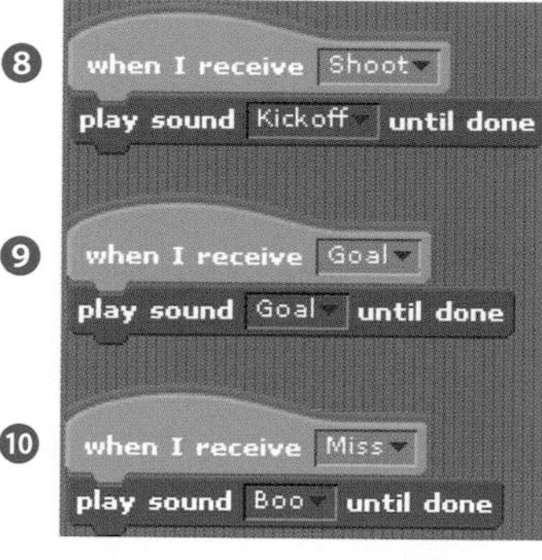

Programs ❽, ❾, and ❿ add sound effects for fun.

```
11
when I receive [Goal]
wait (1) secs
if <(Score) = [5]>
  broadcast [Won] and wait

12
when I receive [Goal]
wait (1) secs
if <<(Ball) = [0]> and <not <(Score) = [5]>>>
  broadcast [Lost] and wait

13
when I receive [Miss]
wait (1) secs
if <(Ball) = [0]>
  broadcast [Lost] and wait
```

Next, we set the rules for winning and losing the game. Program ⓫ will broadcast Won when the Score variable reaches 5. Programs ⓬ and ⓭ will broadcast Lose after all the player's chances are up; that is, when Ball = 0. (Without program ⓭, the player can still lose even if he scores with his last ball.)

Finally, add a Banner sprite with three costumes for the game instructions (Start), the winning screen (Won), and the losing screen (Lost).

Score 5 to win!!

You Won!!

You Lost!!

```
❶ when [flag] clicked
go to x: 0 y: -40
go to front
switch to costume Start
show
wait 0.5 secs
hide

❷ when I receive Won
go to x: 0 y: -55
switch to costume Won
show
stop all

❸ when I receive Lost
go to x: 0 y: -55
switch to costume Lost
show
stop all
```

Then we add these three programs to show the costumes at the right time. Script ❶ shows the Start costume so the player has instructions at the start of the game. The `Won` broadcast will make costume Won appear in script ❷, and the same happens for the Lost costume and `Lost` broadcast in script ❸. The `stop all` block at the end of scripts ❷ and ❸ will stop the game.

Don't forget to save your game before you take on the challenge to show off your soccer skills! Remember: Press the spacebar to kick the ball.

Scratchy's Challenge!!

Can you transform this into a shooting gallery game at an amusement park? How about making Pele a better goalkeeper? Give it a try!

STAGE 6

SCRATCHY'S WILD RIDE

STAGE 6

GOAL!!!
BAM!
THE LOCK IS BROKEN! WHAT AWESOME SOCCER SKILLS!

WELL... I ONLY WON BECAUSE OF EVERYONE'S HELP AND THE DIRECTIONS FROM THE SECRET MANUAL!
DON'T SELL YOURSELF SHORT, MITCH!

PELE'S BACK! ALL THE COSMIC DEFENDERS ARE BACK TOGETHER AGAIN!
LET'S WORK TOGETHER TO RESTORE THE BALANCE OF THE UNIVERSE!

THERE'S A MAGIC GEM IN THE GREAT PYRAMID OF GIZA. WE NEED TO GET IT BEFORE THE DARK WIZARD DOES!

OH NO! WE CAN'T OPEN A STARGATE NEAR THE PYRAMID BECAUSE OF THE MAGIC GEM'S INFLUENCE!
I GUESS WE'LL HAVE TO GET THERE THE OLD-FASHIONED WAY!

THE SAHARA DESERT
THE TRUCK'S READY TO GO. HOP ON, EVERYBODY!

HOLD ON TIGHT!

AHHH!

NO!! THEY TOOK MITCH!
HURRY UP AND START THE CAR! WE HAVE TO CATCH THEM!

DESERT RALLY RACE

STAGE 6

Chapter Focus

Learn how to create a scrolling game, program complex movements for the sprites, and make a background change over time.

Game

Control Scratchy's car to avoid obstacles and to run away from the Dark Minions in order to reach the Great Pyramid of Giza. Each time you crash your car, one of the Cosmic Defenders will jump out. If you crash your car four times, your car will break down!

Let's start by importing a project called *DesertRace*, which already has a bunch of sprites in it. It doesn't have any programs yet, but we'll add some soon.

First, let's look at the Stage. If you click the **Stage** in the Sprite List, you can see that we have a lot of different backgrounds.

6 STAGE

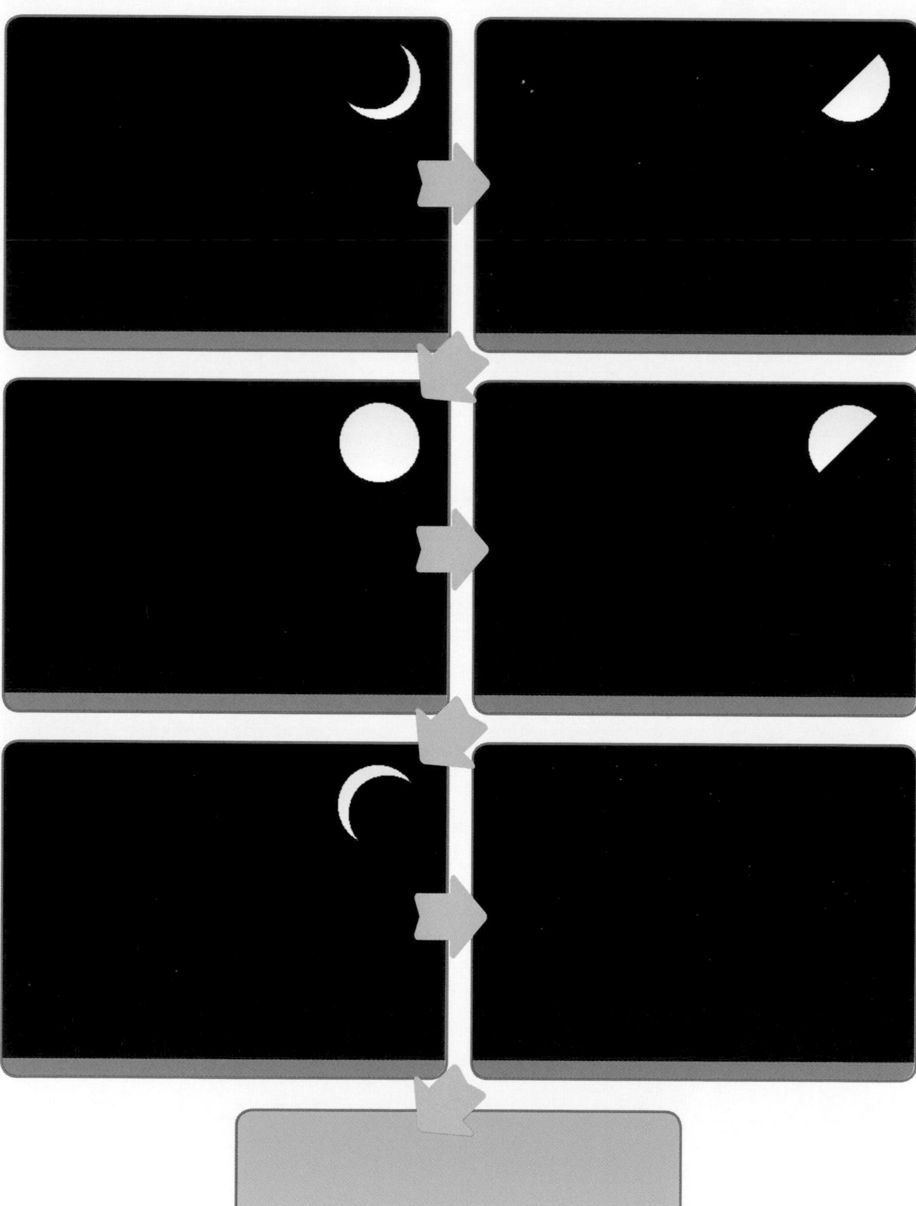

You Win!!

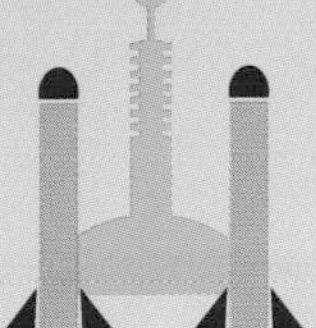

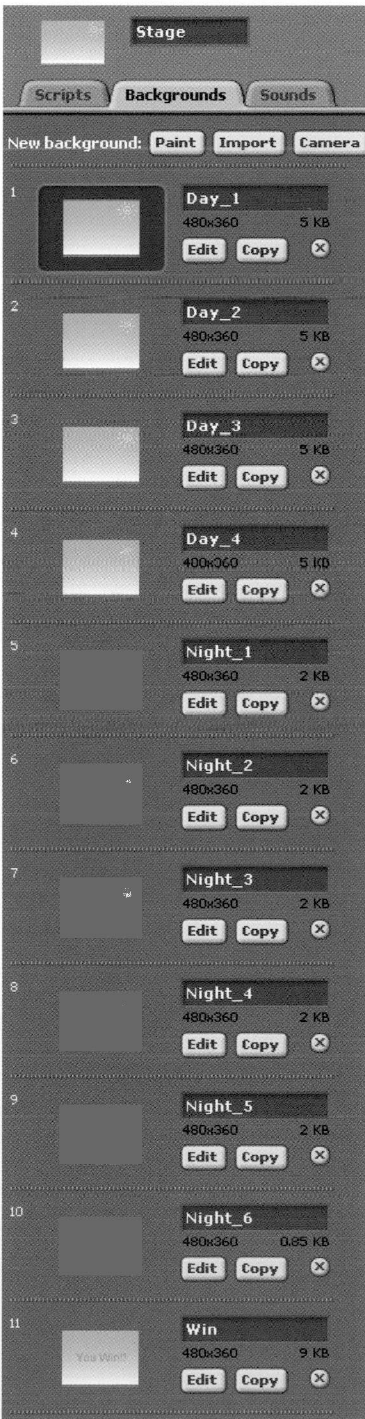

Backgrounds for the Stage are just like costumes for any other kind of sprite. So let's write a program that controls how they change.

Program ❶ will make the background change over time in two loops, day and night. You can use the Duplicate tool to save time with the programming! This animation will give the Stage a cool look as Scratchy drives.

Program ❷ will make the Stage change its background to the Win costume when the `finish` broadcast is received.

❶
```
when [flag] clicked
forever
    repeat 8
        switch to background Day_1
        wait 0.5 secs
        switch to background Day_2
        wait 0.5 secs
        switch to background Day_3
        wait 0.5 secs
        switch to background Day_4
        wait 0.5 secs
    repeat 4
        switch to background Night_1
        wait 0.5 secs
        switch to background Night_2
        wait 0.5 secs
        switch to background Night_3
        wait 0.5 secs
        switch to background Night_4
        wait 0.5 secs
        switch to background Night_5
        wait 0.5 secs
        switch to background Night_6
        wait 0.5 secs
```

❷
```
when I receive finish
switch to background Win
stop all
```

We'll also have the Stage keep track of the time in program ❸. So create a variable called `Time` from the **Variables** palette. We `set Time to 0` and then change it by 1 with each second. We'll use the `Time` variable again later.

❸

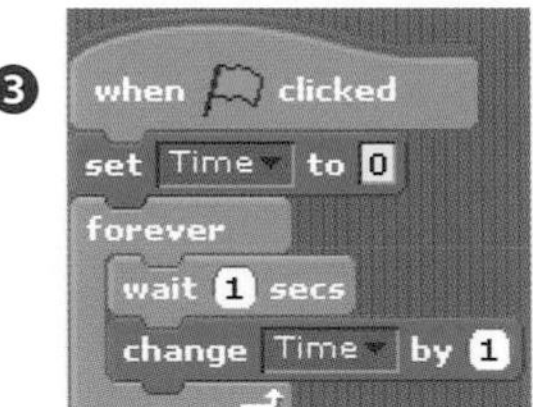

Next, let's look at the road. Try to use the whole width of the Stage if you're drawing it!

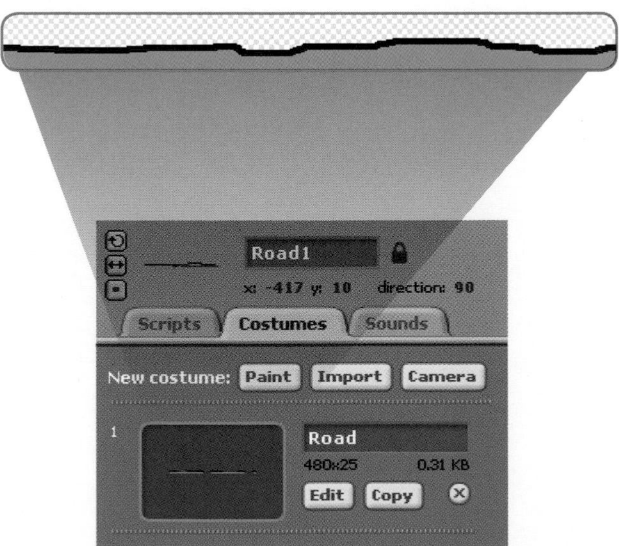

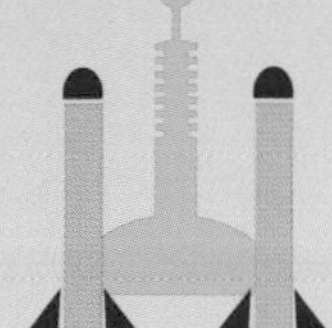

Adding these programs to the Road1 sprite will make it appear on the screen and scroll to the left.

Write program ❶ to make the `Scroll` variable continuously decrease by 1 (that is, `change Scroll by -1`).

Program ❷ will set the road's position. Set the y coordinate to `10` so it won't move up or down, and then add `set x to Scroll` in a `forever` loop. By doing this, the road will continuously move to the left as the `Scroll` variable changes.

Program ❸ will make the `Scroll` variable reset to a 0 value once it reaches a value less than -479.

Tip: Why did we use the number -479? The width of the entire Scratch Stage is 480 pixels, so that's when it will roll off the Stage.

Now duplicate the Road1 sprite to create a second sprite called Road2.

Add this program to use the `Scroll` variable from the first road sprite. This time, we use a trick to make Road2 follow right behind Road1. By setting the x coordinate to `Scroll + 480`, we know Road2 will always follow behind Road1. This means that the player always has a road to drive on, no matter what!

Next, add Scratchy's Car sprite.

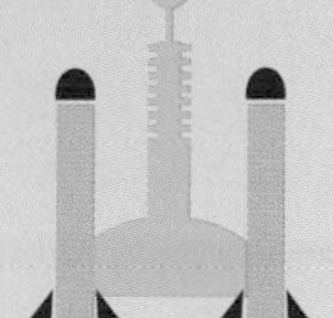

Program ❶ for the Car does a lot of work. First, it sets the costume, size, and position.

The `forever` loop holds the rest of the program. The `change y by -5` block will pull the car down, giving it gravity. The `if touching color` block makes the car bounce up whenever it touches the black part of the road, making it seem like they're driving on a very bumpy road. The `if key up arrow pressed?` block will broadcast `jump` and then wait.

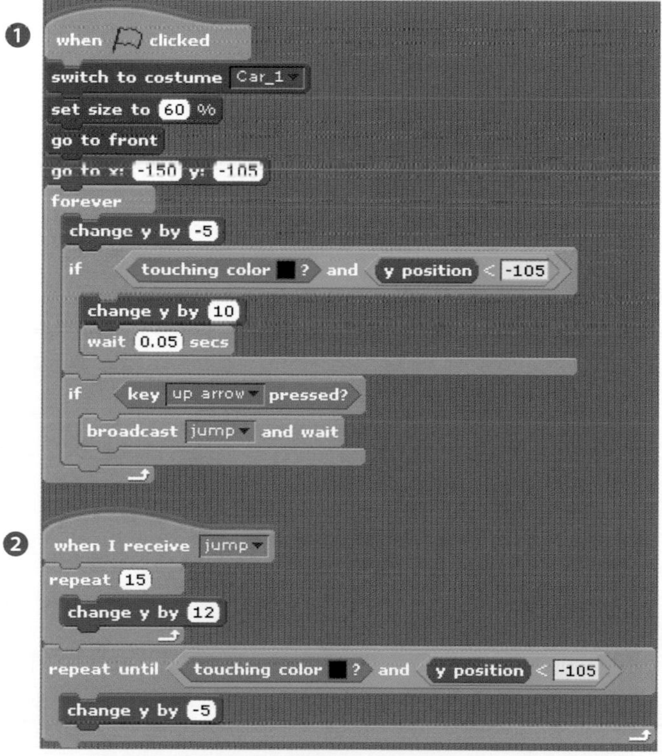

Program ❷ makes the car "listen" for the `jump` broadcast and makes the car jump up.

The `broadcast jump and wait` block in program ❶ will temporarily stop the first program so the second program can run.

Now add program ❸ so that the car can move left and right.

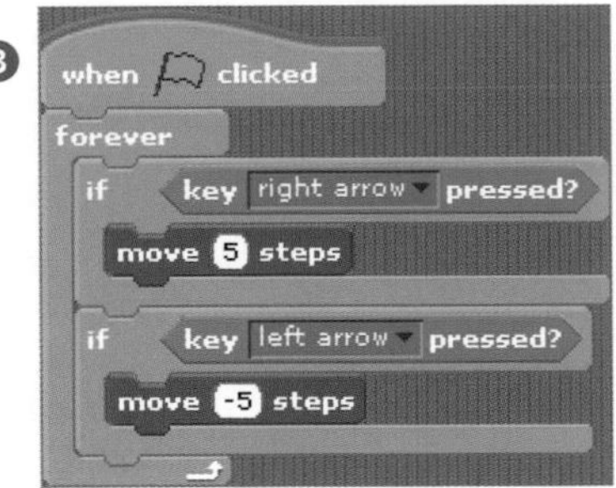

In program ❹, we add some speech bubbles as instructions for the player.

In program ❺, we create a new variable called `Life`. When the `Life` value is less than 1, we'll set the car's costume to Boom! and then end the game with the `stop all` command.

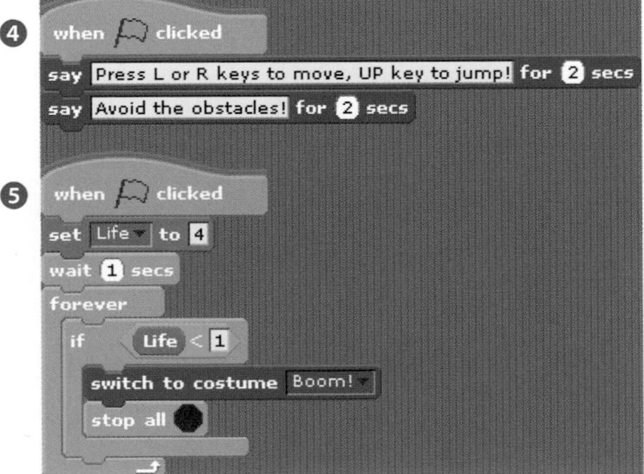

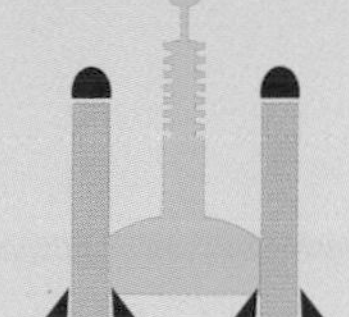

Once you're finished with the Car sprite's programming, you can add some passengers—the Cosmic Defenders!

Add these three sprites, and then drag them onto the car. Gobo is at the back, Fabu is in the middle, and Pele is in the front. It's okay if they overlap a bit.

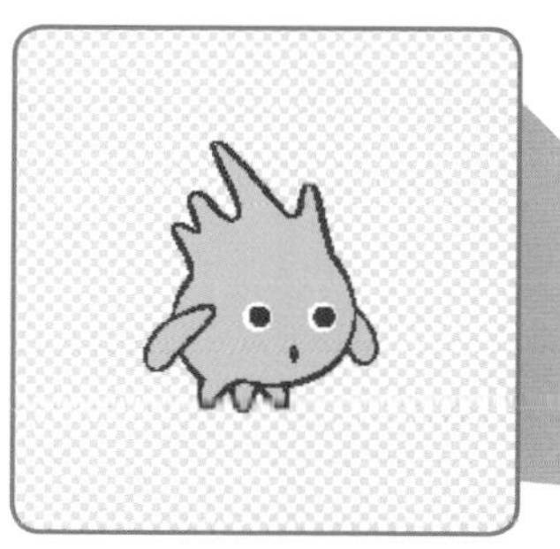

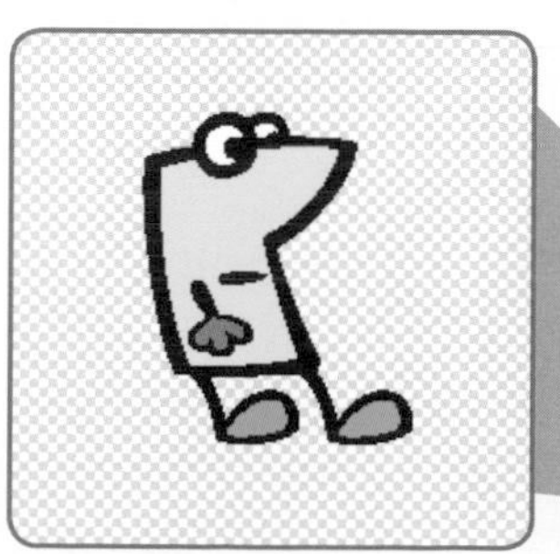

Write this program for Gobo. It sets his size and position and uses the `go to` block so he'll always follow the Car sprite. Once the variable Life drops to less than 4 (`Life < 4`), he'll shoot to a random area. When he touches the top of the screen (`y position = 180`), we make him disappear by using the `hide` block.

```
Gobo
x: -150 y: -105 direction: 90
Scripts | Costumes | Sounds

when [flag] clicked
set size to 30 %
go to front
go back 1 layers
show
point in direction 90
go to Car
forever
    repeat until Life < 4
        change y by 10
        wait 0.05 secs
        go to Car
    point in direction pick random 15 to 345
    glide 1 secs to x: pick random 250 to -250 y: 180
    if y position = 180
        hide
    hide
```

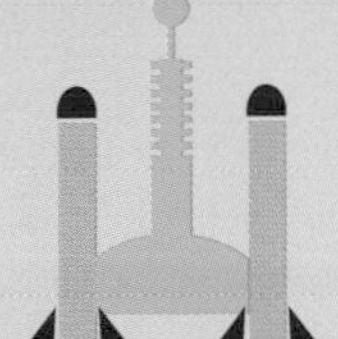

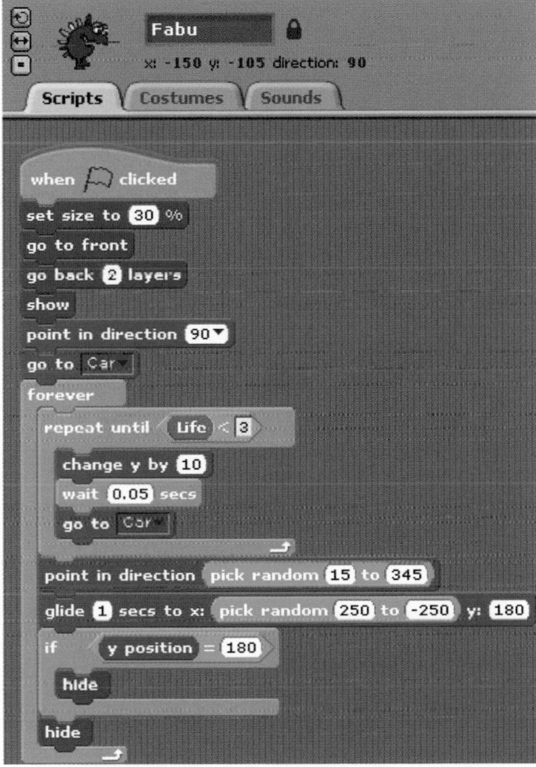

Drag and copy Gobo's program onto Fabu in the Sprite List. You'll need to change only a few things. Most important, change the `repeat until` block to `Life < 3`, so Fabu will bounce out at a different time.

Do the same thing for Pele, but change the `Life` value to 2. Because Pele's sprite is a little bigger than the others, we also set his size to 25%.

```
Pele
x: -150 y: -105 direction: 90
Scripts | Costumes | Sounds

when clicked
set size to 25 %
go to front
go back 3 layers
show
point in direction 90
go to Car
forever
    repeat until Life < 2
        change y by 10
        wait 0.05 secs
        go to Car
    point in direction pick random 15 to 345
    glide 1 secs to x: pick random 250 to -250 y: 180
    if y position = 180
        hide
    hide
```

Now we can add the programming for the obstacles. First, let's take a look at the thorny and dangerous Bush! It has two costumes.

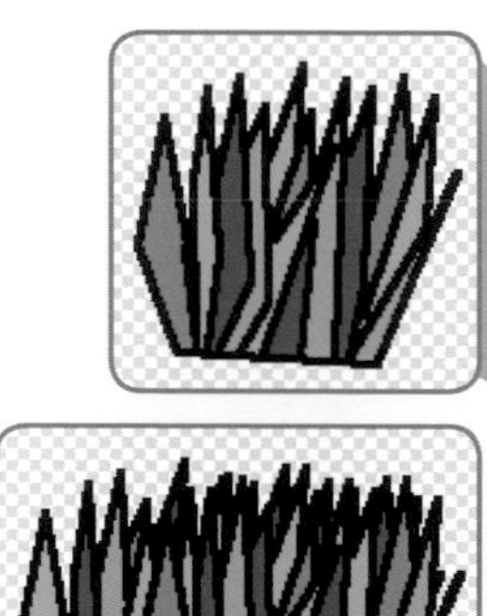

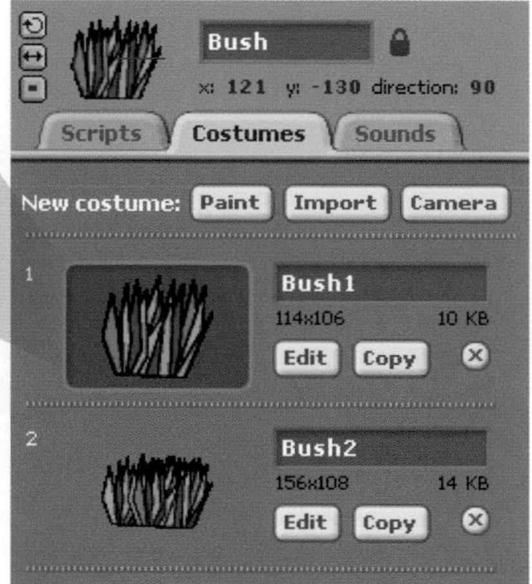

And then write these three programs:

Program ❶ controls when the bush appears and makes sure it moves with the road. Once it touches the left edge of the screen, it'll disappear and switch to the next bush costume.

Program ❷ programs the Car to `change Life by -1` (that is, lose one life) whenever it touches an obstacle. Notice how we programmed the computer to check if the player still has enough `Life` value left using the `and` and `not` blocks.

And program ❸ makes the bush disappear once it receives the `finish` signal, which ends the game.

❶
```
when [flag] clicked
switch to costume Bush1
hide
forever
    wait 8 secs
    go to x: 230 y: -130
    show
    repeat until x position < -230
        change x by -1
    hide
    next costume
```

❷
```
when [flag] clicked
wait 1 secs
forever
    if touching Car ? and not Life = 0
        change Life by -1
        wait 6 secs
```

❸
```
when I receive finish
hide
```

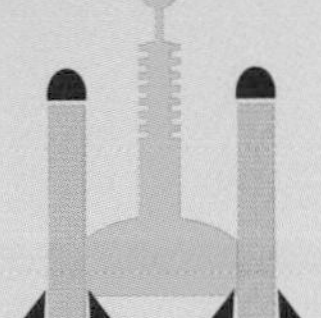

Now let's look at the Tower sprite, which also has two costumes. This obstacle will be tough to jump!

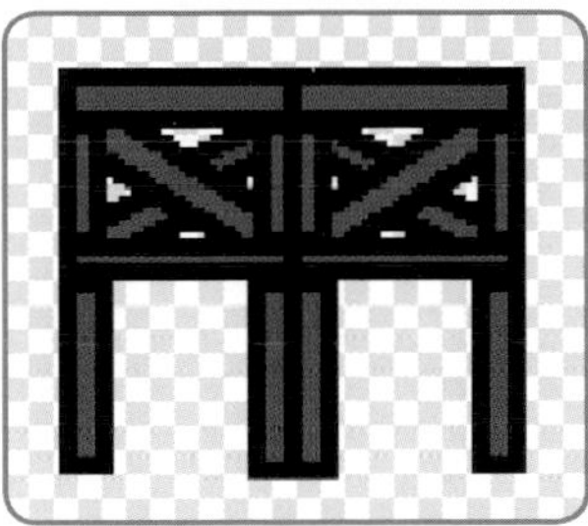

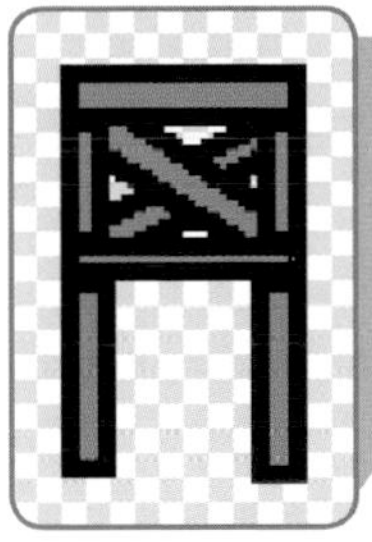

```
when [flag] clicked
switch to costume [Tower1]
hide
forever
    wait (18) secs
    go to x: (230) y: (-130)
    show
    repeat until <(x position) < (-230)>
        change x by (-1)
    hide
    next costume

when [flag] clicked
wait (1) secs
forever
    if <<touching [Car]?> and <not <(Life) = (0)>>>
        change [Life] by (-1)
        wait (6) secs

when I receive [finish]
hide
```

We can once again copy the program we created for the bushes. Edit the costume name and the time it appears, and you're good to go!

Create a new sprite for Legs, the evil octopus Dark Minion. But don't you think it's a little boring just to have one image for him?

Why don't we try animating him?

In the Paint Editor, use the **Select** tool to grab the end of his tentacle.

Next, click this button to flip his arm up and then drag it back into place.

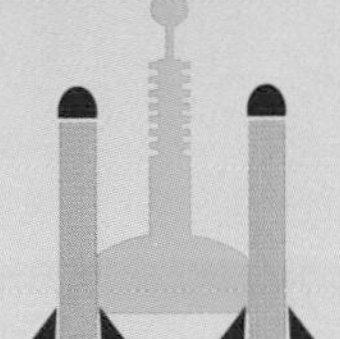

Do the same for his other tentacles, and there you go—a new look!

Tip: Editing existing costumes is an easy way to animate a character without having to redraw it. The Select and Rotate tools let you quickly change the position of a sprite's arms and legs.

Now let's get back to programming! Program ❶ makes Legs switch between his two costumes in a forever loop. Program ❷ makes him hide when he receives the finish broadcast.

Programs ❸ and ❹ control Legs's movements and make him an unpredictable obstacle for Scratchy's car.

❸

```
when flag clicked
set size to 50 %
hide
forever
    wait pick random 15 to 20 secs
    go to x: 230 y: 70
    show
    repeat until x position < -230
        change x by -3
    hide
```

❹

```
when flag clicked
forever
    repeat 10
        change y by -5
        wait 0.05 secs
    repeat 10
        change y by 5
        wait 0.05 secs
```

Lastly, program ❺ for Legs adds a condition that will subtract life points from the `Life` variable, just as with the Bush and Tower obstacles.

❺
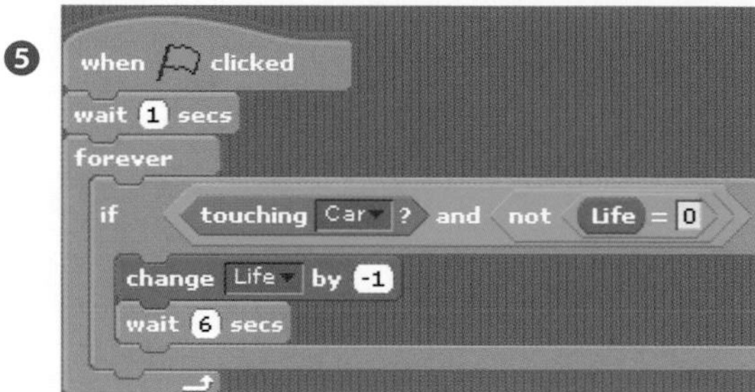

And now we'll move on to the final sprite of the game: Egypt's Great Pyramid of Giza!

Let's start with this photo:

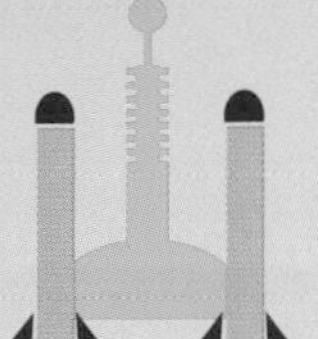

By adding this sprite, we'll make it look like Scratchy is "arriving" at the pyramids. Edit the Giza costume so that the cool backgrounds will show through and so that the bottom matches the orange of the road. Now we can make the photo fit into our existing game.

Giza
x: 0 y: -75 direction: 90
Scripts | Costumes | Sounds
New costume: Paint | Import | Camera
1 Giza 480x196 126 KB
Edit | Copy

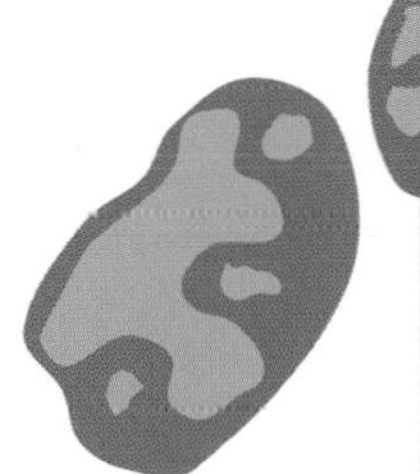

Write a script so that the pyramid slowly appears from the right, after the game is run for 60 seconds. Once it reaches the center of the screen (`x position = 0`), it broadcasts the `finish` signal. When the other sprites receive this signal, the game ends.

```
when [flag] clicked
switch to costume Giza
set size to 70 %
hide
wait until Time = 60
show
go to x: 350 y: -75
repeat until x position = 0
    change x by -1
broadcast finish and wait
```

After saving your file, board Scratchy's speedy car and drive into the Sahara Desert to begin your wild adventure!

Scratchy's Challenge!!

Can you use these programs to create another scrolling game? Give it try! (Tip: The height of Scratch's screen is 360 pixels.) Make the game even more challenging by having the car go really fast!

THE LOST TREASURES OF GIZA

7 STAGE

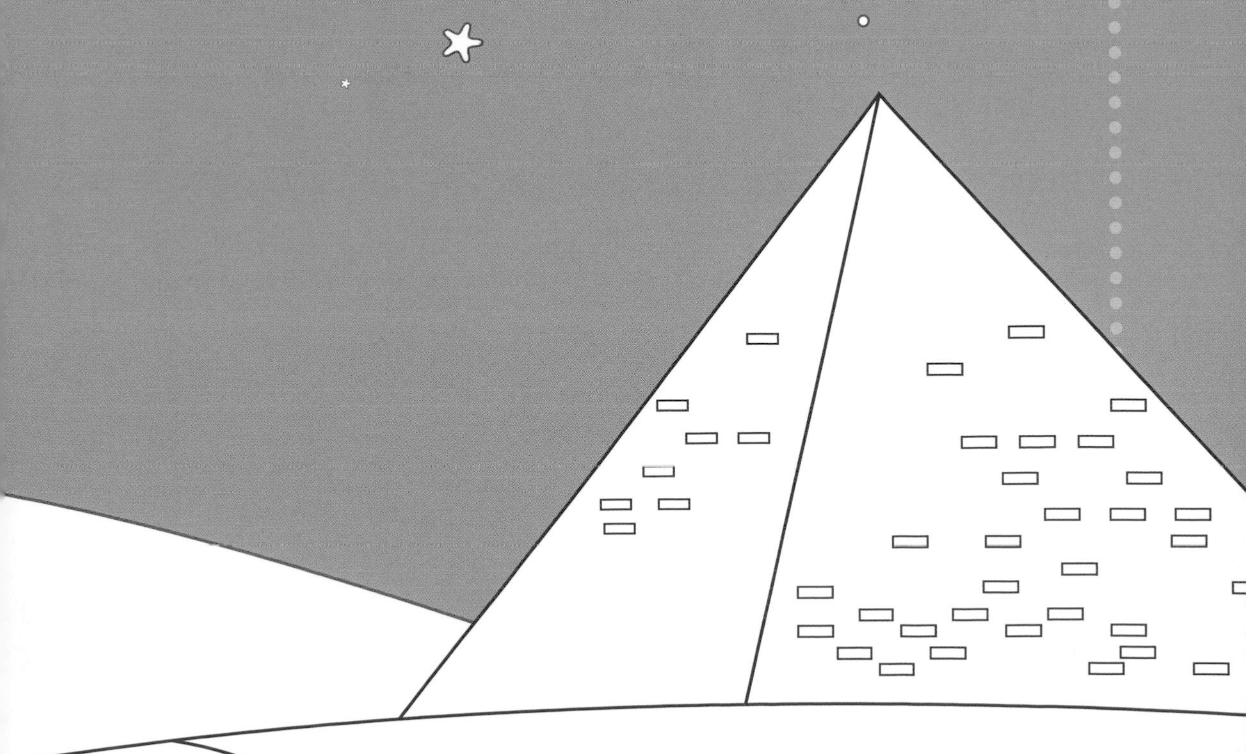

STAGE 7

THERE'S THE GREAT PYRAMID OF GIZA!

SNIFF WE TRIED OUR BEST, BUT THEY STILL GOT AWAY!
WHAT WILL WE DO WITHOUT MITCH'S PROGRAMMING?

DON'T GIVE UP! THERE HAS TO BE A WAY!

WE CAN TEACH SCRATCHY HOW TO USE THE SECRET MANUAL!

OH! AND IF WE FIND THE MAGIC GEM, MAYBE WE CAN GET MITCH BACK!
WELL THEN, I GUESS WE SHOULD GIVE YOU THE POWER!

BZZT BZZT

THANKS, GUYS! I KNOW HOW TO USE IT NOW!

THERE ARE A LOT OF TRAPS IN THERE. YOU MUST BE CAREFUL!
NO MATTER WHAT, DON'T GIVE UP!

SIGH AND I THOUGHT EGYPTIANS LIKED CATS.

ESCAPE THE MAZE!

STAGE 7

Chapter Focus

Learn how to design an interactive maze with a guard, booby traps, and treasure!

Game

Guide Scratchy through the maze, and into the treasure room to collect the Magic Gem. After he picks up the Magic Gem, other traps in the pyramid are sprung, and he must escape!

For this game, begin by importing a project file called *Maze*, instead of starting with a blank project. This project file has all the images you need for the game, but none of the sprites have any programs yet.

Take a look around, and especially take notice of the Stage. You can see that all of the walls in our maze have the same orange color. We'll use that color as the boundary, so Scratchy can't walk through walls!

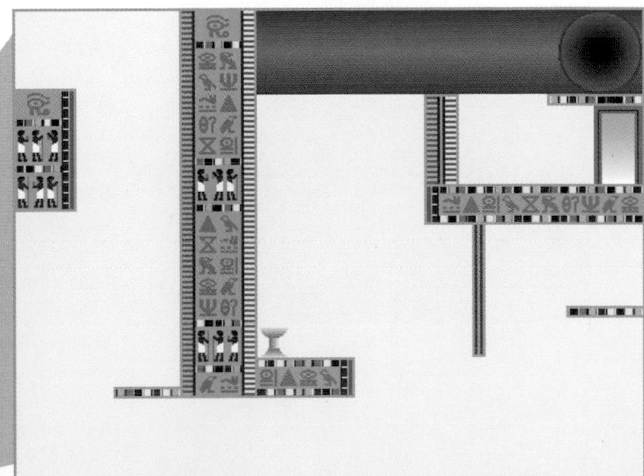

STAGE 7

Click the sprite for Scratchy called **Indy-Cat** in the Sprite List. Then click the **Sounds** tab and add a sound effect for him. Either record a "meow" yourself or import the Cat sound effect. We'll add a program to make Scratchy meow whenever he bumps into a bad guy or trap.

Let's begin by thinking about how the game should start and how the player will win at the end of the game.

Program ❶ gives the player the instructions for the game using the say block. Now when the game starts, the player will know he needs to grab the Magic Gem to win.

And, of course, to end the game, Scratchy needs to escape the maze with the Magic Gem. Now let's write a program for the end of the game. Program ❷ uses a special kind of block within a forever if loop. If Scratchy touches the color blue—that is, the blue sky of the exit door—he'll say "Yeah!!" and broadcast Won, which will cause the game to end. (Because the maze itself doesn't have any blue, we don't have to worry about ending the game accidentally.)

To write program ❷, drag the touching color command from the **Sensing** palette into the if block. Click the color inside the block, and an eyedropper appears. Click the blue of the doorway, and you're all set. We'll use the touching color command for another neat programming trick next.

Now take a look at program ❸. It looks pretty complicated, but it's really not so hard. Can you tell what it does just by reading it?

First, we set the direction and position of Scratchy. That's simple enough. But what about the big `forever` loop? That holds all of the rest of the program, and that's how we'll program Scratchy's movements. First, if you press the up key, you can see there's a command that will `change y by 3`. But then *inside* that `if` loop, there's a second `if` loop!

If Scratchy is touching orange, the computer tells Scratchy to `change y by -3`. What's that all about? Well, did you notice that the walls of the maze are all orange? So if Scratchy bumps into the orange wall, we want the wall to stop him. And what does 3 + (-3) equal? That's right, 0. So when Scratchy touches the orange wall, he doesn't change his y position at all. He won't move! Cool.

The down, left, and right `if` loops work in just the same way, and they have a second `if` loop inside them as well. Make sure to pick orange with the eyedropper for every `if touching color` command.

Now Scratchy can't walk through the maze's walls or gates. Notice that the edge of the Stage has a thin band of orange, too. Scratchy can't walk off the Stage either! He's trapped in our maze, just like we want.

❸

```
when clicked
point in direction 90
go to x: -205 y: 150
go to front
go back 1 layers
forever
    if key up arrow pressed?
        change y by 3
        if touching color ?
            change y by -3
    if key down arrow pressed?
        change y by -3
        if touching color ?
            change y by 3
    if key left arrow pressed?
        point in direction -90
        change x by -3
        if touching color ?
            change x by 3
    if key right arrow pressed?
        point in direction 90
        change x by 3
        if touching color ?
            change x by -3
```

Finally, for program ❹, we use the `forever if` block and the `or` block to program what will happen whenever Scratchy bumps into a trap or a bad guy. A speech bubble will say "Oh!", the sound effect Cat will play, and Scratchy returns to his starting position.

Tip: The second `say` block is blank. This makes the "Oh!" disappear.

❹

```
when clicked
wait 1 secs
forever if touching Turnstile ? or touching Whiptail ? or touching Wall_L ? or touching Wall_R ? or touching Stone ?
    say Oh!
    play sound Cat
    glide 1 secs to x: -205 y: 150
    say
```

7
STAGE

Now is a good time to make sure that your programs work as you expected. Click 🏴, and make sure Scratchy moves up, down, left, and right. Try bumping into the walls of the maze. Does Scratchy stop moving once he hits a wall in all four directions? If not, go back and double-check your programming. (Remember that if Scratchy touches the orange wall, his movement should add up to 0.) Try hitting an obstacle or a bad guy to make sure Scratchy returns to the start of the maze.

Next, click the sprite for **Whiptail**, the Dark Minion guarding the pyramid. Add a program that sets his size and starting position and then makes him pace back and forth in the maze.

Whiptail
x: 166 y: -145 direction: 90
Scripts | Costumes | Sounds
New costume: Paint Import Camera
1 Whiptail 180x126 5 KB Edit Copy

```
when 🏴 clicked
set size to 40 %
go to x: -195 y: -145
forever
  point in direction 90
  glide 5 secs to x: 180 y: -145
  wait 2 secs
  point in direction -90
  glide 5 secs to x: -195 y: -145
  wait 2 secs
```

Then click the **Turnstile** sprite, and add a program to make it spin using the `turn` block. The sprite doesn't move around at all, so we just need to set one position.

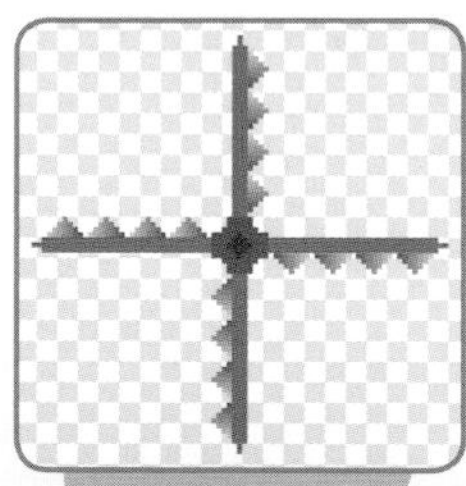

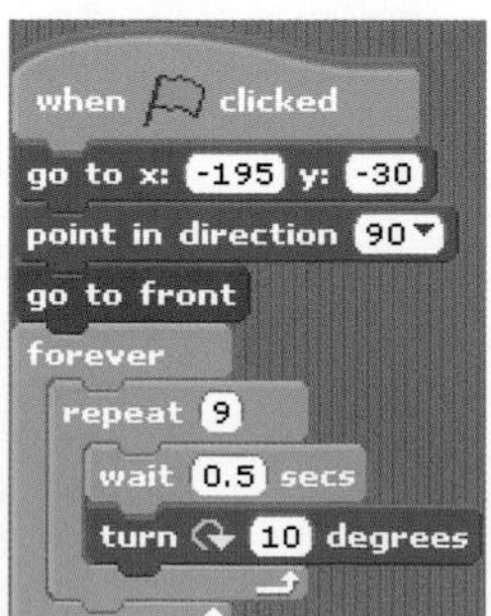

Turnstile
x: -195 y: -30 direction: -120
Scripts | Costumes | Sounds
New costume: Paint Import Camera
1 Turnstile 81x81 2 KB Edit Copy

At this point, take a look at the Lock and Key sprites, which are circled in blue below. Scratchy will need to pick up the Key first, in order to open the Lock. Let's add some programs for them next.

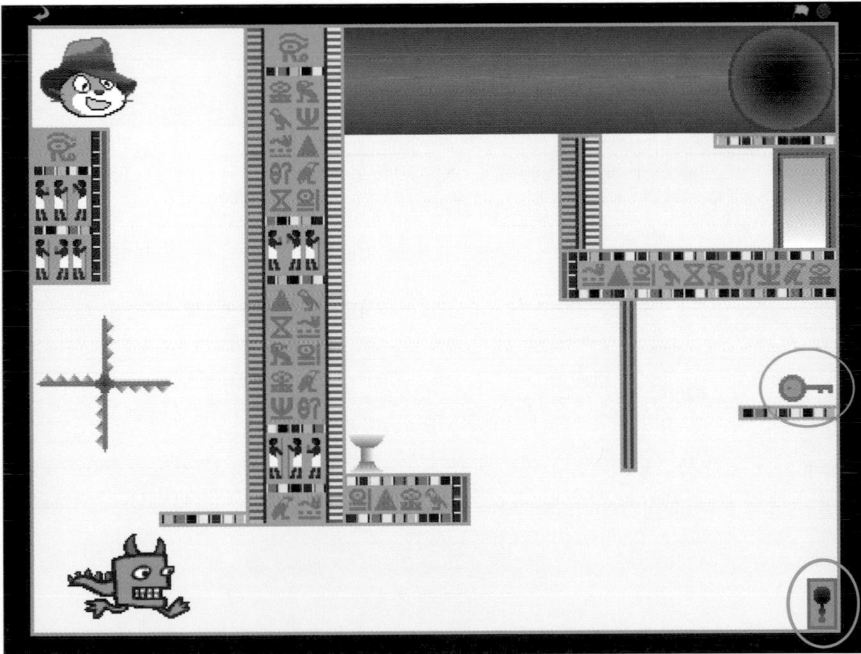

First, click the **Lock** in the Sprite List to give it a simple program—this just sets its location in the maze. The program that actually opens the gate is in the Key sprite.

STAGE 7

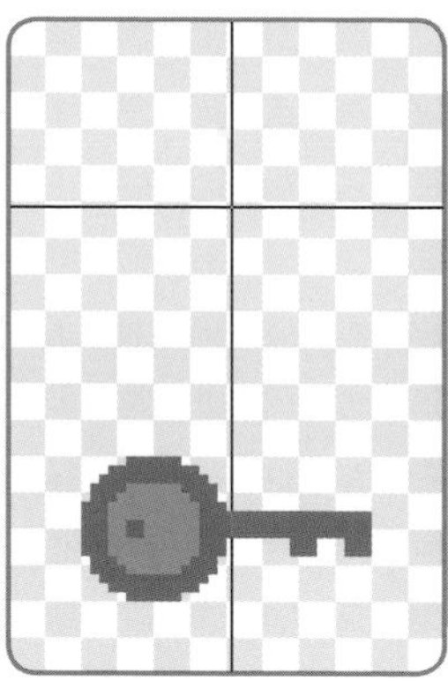

Tip: When creating the Key sprite, use the **Set Costume Center** button in the Paint Editor to make sure Scratchy and the Key don't overlap.

Click the **Key** in the Sprite List, and add a sound in the **Sounds** tab. Then click the **Scripts** tab to add this program. We want a sound to play when Scratchy picks up the Key and then have the Key follow Scratchy, using the go to command. When the Key touches the Lock, the Gate Open signal is broadcast.

Now to program the Gate sprite. Because it has an orange border just like our maze, Scratchy can't enter the treasure room unless it moves!

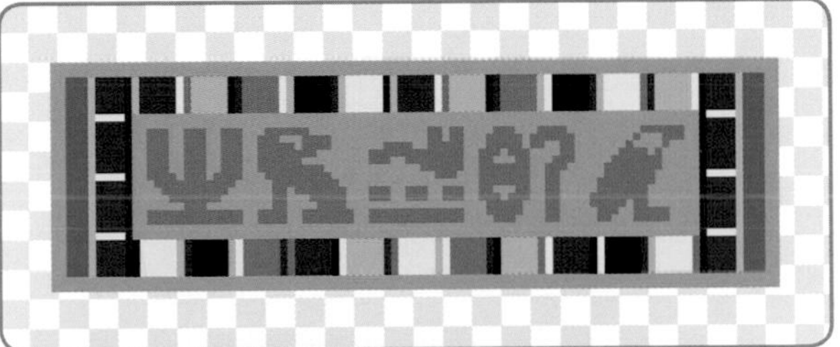

Click the **Gate** in the Sprite List, and then add the DirtyWhir sound to the Gate in its **Sounds** tab.

Now add some programs. Program ❶ just sets the Gate's location. Program ❷ makes the Gate glide out of the way when the `Gate Open` broadcast signal is received. Program ❸ plays a sound effect.

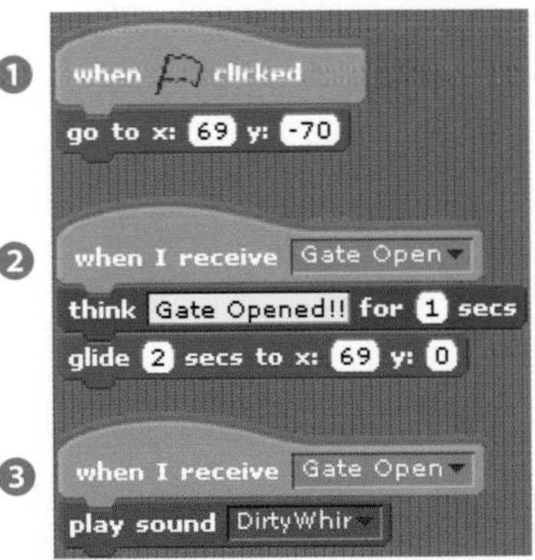

If you haven't tried out the game yet, give it a test now by clicking ! See if you can get Scratchy to enter the treasure room.

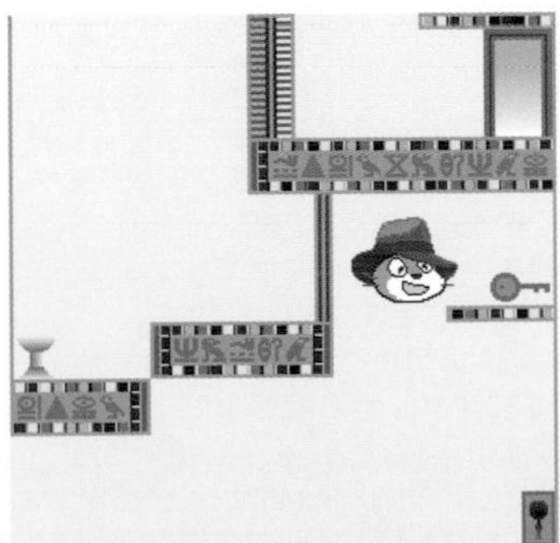

STAGE 7

Next, let's program the Magic Gem sprite. We'll give it a sound effect called Fairydust in the **Sounds** tab.

If it's not already there, you can just drag the sprite on top of its stand on the Stage.

❶
```
when [flag] clicked
clear graphic effects
forever
    change [color] effect by 25
```

❷
```
when [flag] clicked
go to x: -42 y: -48
show
wait until < touching [Indy-Cat] ? >
play sound [Fairydust]
think [Gem Obtained!!] for 1 secs
broadcast [Stone]
hide
```

Then write two programs for it. Program ❶ makes the Magic Gem change colors. Program ❷ sets the Magic Gem's position and then uses a `wait until` block to determine what happens when Scratchy grabs the Magic Gem. When Scratchy touches the Magic Gem, it broadcasts Stone. This will release the final traps in the maze!

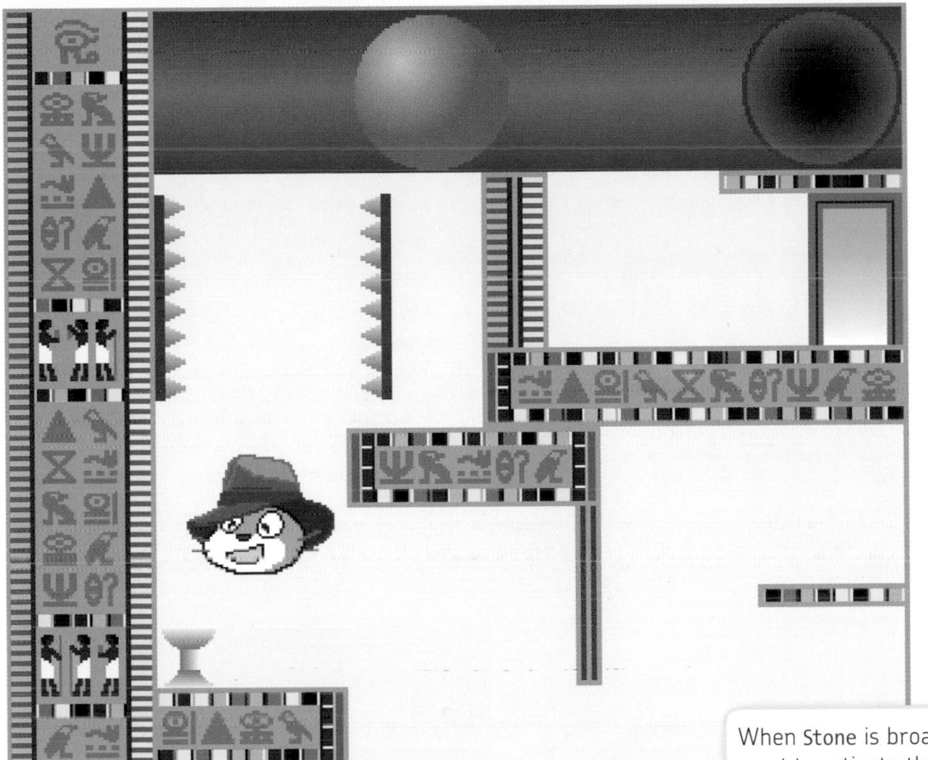

When Stone is broadcast, we want to activate the rolling stone and the spiked wall traps.

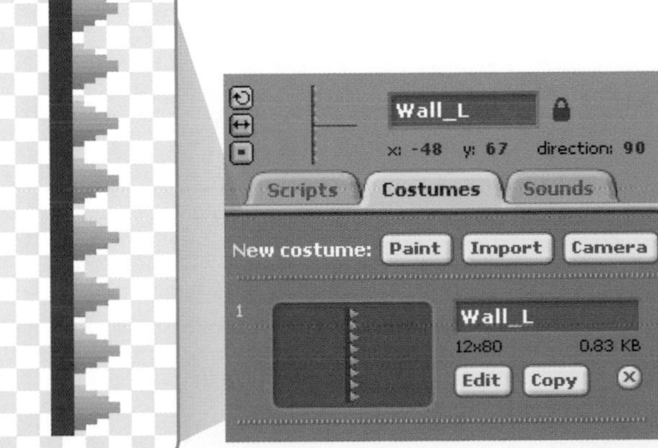

Our spiked wall trap will actually be two different sprites. Wall_L (the left side of the trap) gets one simple program to set its position.

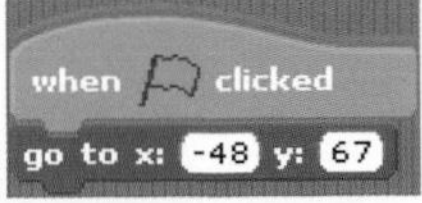

STAGE 7

The right side has its own sprite called Wall_R. Add these two programs to set the position and make it move. This wall listens for the Stone broadcast and begins to glide back and forth, most dangerously!

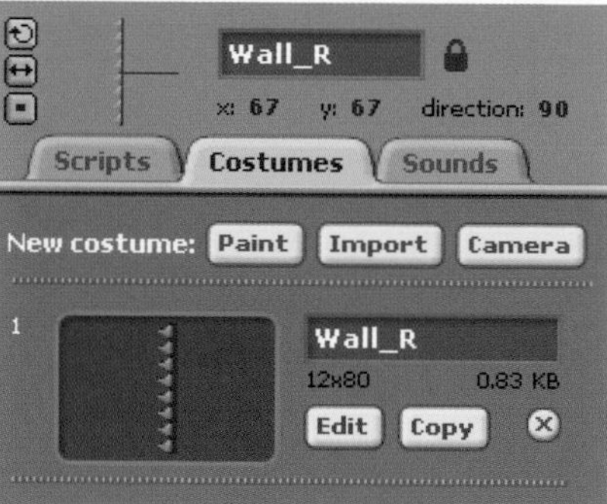

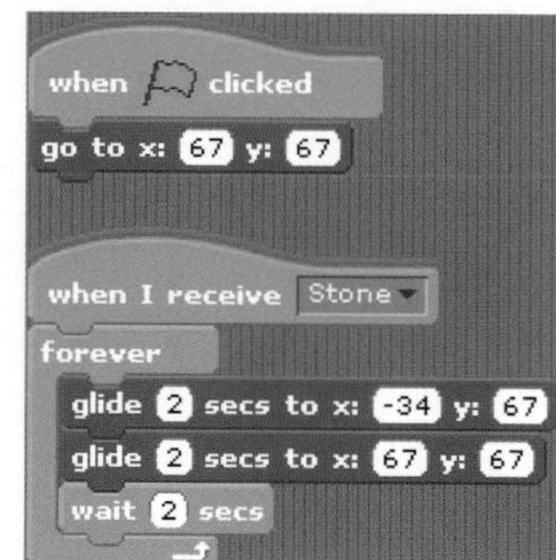

Waiting outside the passage is a rolling boulder sprite called Stone. I've used different shades of gray for the Stone to give it a 3D look.

```
❶ when [flag] clicked
  hide
  forever
    turn ↻ 10 degrees

❷ when I receive Stone
  forever
    go to x: -39 y: 146
    show
    glide 4 secs to x: 206 y: 146
    hide
```

Program ❶ for the Stone will make the sprite appear to roll, giving it a realistic animation. Program ❷ controls the movement of the Stone—it rolls down the passage and then appears again at the start, in a forever loop.

Finally, we have a sprite for the winning screen called Won.

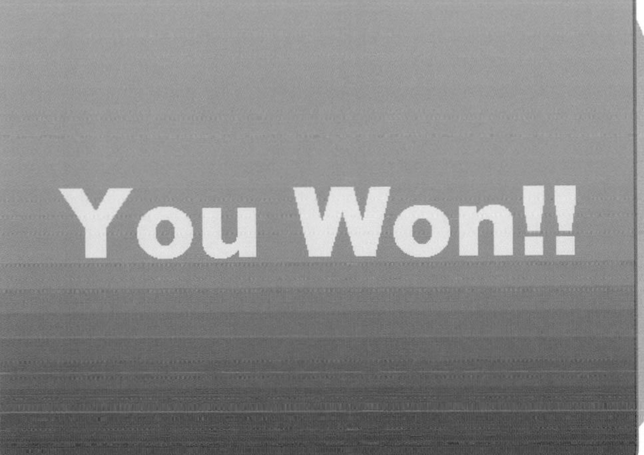

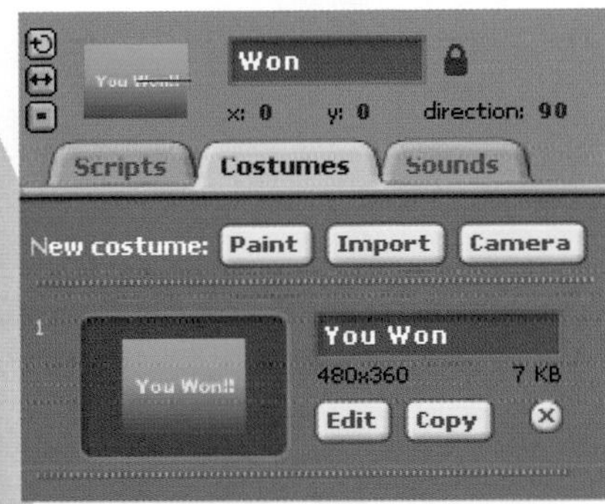

```
❶
when [flag] clicked
hide

❷
when I receive [Won]
go to x: 0 y: 0
go to front
show

❸
when I receive [Won]
play sound [Won] until done
stop all
```

Add these three short programs. Program ❶ hides the sprite, and program ❷ displays it only when it receives `Won`. Program ❸ plays the sound effect we added in the **Sounds** tab.

Tip: The `stop all` command in program ❸ will make the Stone, Whiptail, and all other sprites stop moving.

Wondering where that `Won` broadcast will come from? Remember that Scratchy broadcasts `Won` when he touches the blue in the doorway. We added that way back in program ❷ on page 100. So we're finished! Yes!

7 STAGE

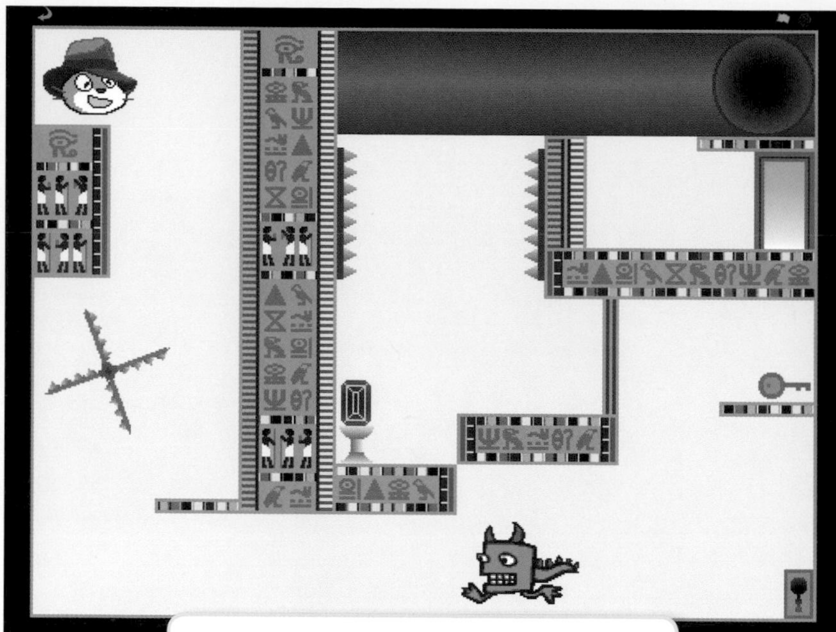

Save your project so you don't lose any of your work! Now help Scratchy collect the Magic Gem and escape from the dangerous maze.

Scratchy's Challenge!!

By making the sprites smaller, you can create an even more complicated maze with more traps. Or you could add a second player and make it a race to the finish! Give it a try!

STAGE 8

WIZARD'S RACE!

STAGE 8

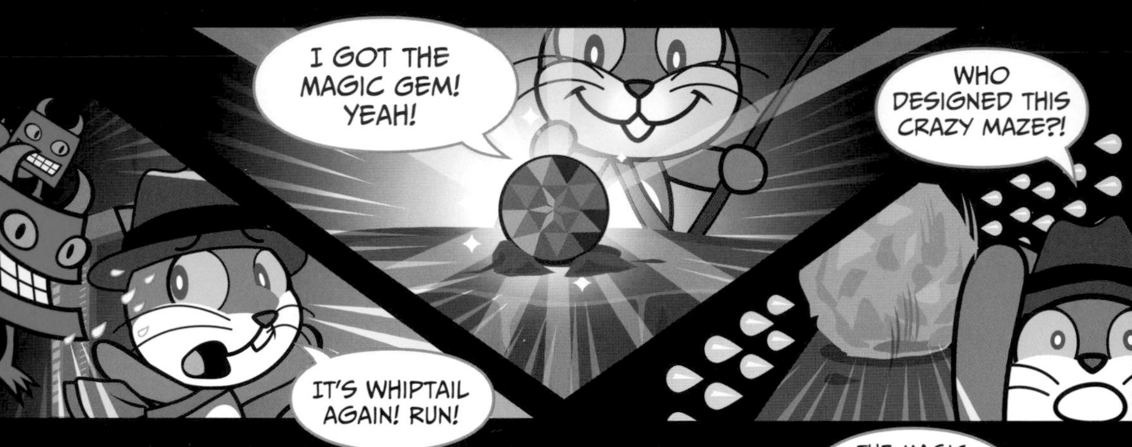

I GOT THE MAGIC GEM! YEAH!
IT'S WHIPTAIL AGAIN! RUN!
WHO DESIGNED THIS CRAZY MAZE?!

WHEW. I GOT IT, GUYS!
MAGIC PORTAL!
WOW, WHERE ARE WE?

THE MAGIC GEM BROUGHT US TO THE LAND OF MAGIC.
RATA? WHY ARE YOU HELPING US?

NEVER MIND ABOUT THAT. USE THIS MAGIC BROOM TO RACE TO THE SECOND GEM BEFORE THE DARK WIZARD GETS IT!
THIS BROOM IS AN OLD MODEL, SO YOU'LL NEED TO WAVE YOUR WAND TO MAKE IT GO FAST!
MEOW! THANKS FOR THE TIP.

SORCEROR'S CHALLENGE

STAGE 8

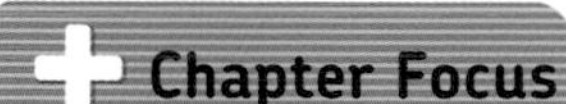

Chapter Focus

Learn how to control the Stage with multiple costumes, play music with Scratch, and create other animations.

The Game

This is a simple "button-mashing" game. Rapidly press two keys back and forth to make Scratchy fly. He needs to beat all three levels within 15 seconds to collect the second Magic Gem.

Start by opening the Scratch project *WizardsRace*. This project file has all the sprites you'll need, but it doesn't have any programs yet. We can customize how it looks later. For now, we'll focus on the programming.

First, let's take a look at the Stage. It has three backgrounds. We'll use these as levels for Scratchy's ride on the broomstick.

Write program ❶ for the Stage to sets its first background. Program ❷ changes the Stage's background when it receives the next level broadcast.

Tip: You'll need to choose **new...** in the dropdown menu of the when I receive block to create the next level broadcast.

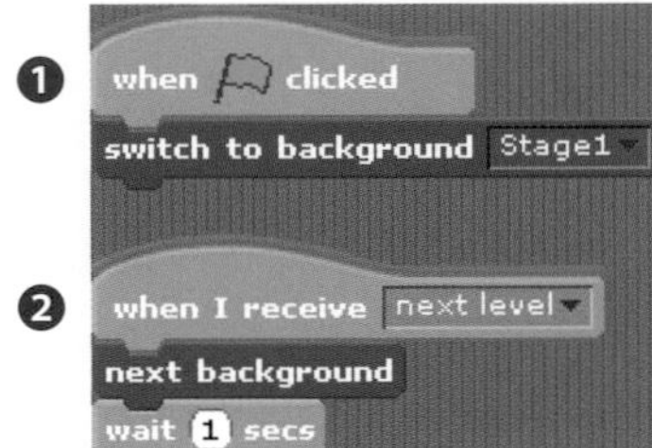

Create a LEVEL variable, and then add programs ❸ and ❹. Program ❸ makes sure that we start at level 1. Program ❹ listens for the next level broadcast from program ❹ on page 116 and increases the LEVEL variable by 1.

```
❺ when [flag] clicked
  set TIME to 15.0

❻ when I receive Start
  reset timer
  forever
    set TIME to (15 - timer)
    if (TIME < 0)
      broadcast LOSE
```

Create a second variable called TIME, and then add program ❺, which gives you 15 seconds to complete the race. Program ❻ broadcasts LOSE when you've run out of time.

Hint: Program ❻ has a couple tricky things in it. First, you'll need to create a new Start broadcast in the when I receive block. The script also makes use of Scratch's built-in timer variable and uses some special commands from the **Operators**, **Sensing**, and **Variables** palettes. You need to use the reset timer block in program ❻, as Scratch's timer starts just as soon as you open the project. This command will let you try the game again after you've lost, too.

Next, we'll program the sprite for Scratchy the wizard. The sprite is called Harry-Catter and has two costumes. We'll give him two sound effects, too, in the **Sounds** tab.

Then write program ❶ to set his starting costume and position. Program ❷ makes him float up and down.

```
❶
when [flag] clicked
go to x: -135 y: 65
switch to costume HarryCatter2
go to front

❷
when [flag] clicked
forever
    change y by 2
    wait 0.3 secs
    change y by -2
    wait 0.3 secs
```

Program ❸ controls how Scratchy moves. The player will need to press the left and right arrow keys, one after another, to move Scratchy.

❸
```
when I receive [Start]
forever
  if <<key [left arrow] pressed?> and <key [right arrow] pressed?>>
    move (0) steps
  if <<key [left arrow] pressed?> and <not <key [right arrow] pressed?>>>
    switch to costume [HC-2]
    move (10) steps
    wait until <<key [right arrow] pressed?> and <not <key [left arrow] pressed?>>>
    switch to costume [HC-4]
    move (10) steps
```

Can you see how this program works? The player can start with either the right or left arrow. The not block makes sure the player doesn't "cheat" by pressing both the right and left arrow keys at the same time.

❹
```
when I receive [Start]
repeat (2)
  wait until <touching [Magic] ?>
  play sound [Fairydust]
  play sound [Zoom]
  broadcast [next level]
  go to x: (-135) y: (65)
  say [Next Level!] for (0.5) secs
say [Get the Magic Gem!] for (1) secs
wait until <touching [Magic] ?>
broadcast [WIN]
```

Finally, write program ❹ so that once Scratchy reaches the Magic sprite, sound effects will play, `next level` is broadcast, and Scratchy says "Next Level!" Remember that the `next level` broadcast will make the Stage change backgrounds.

After that loop repeats twice, the player is on the third level. Scratchy will now say "Get the Magic Gem!" and broadcast `WIN` if he reaches the Magic sprite in time.

Now let's take a look at the costumes for Magic, the sprite that is our Magic Gate and the Magic Gem. The sprite will appear on the right of the Stage, and it will serve as Scratchy's goal for each of the three levels.

Here are those costumes for this sprite. We'll change costumes with each level, with the Magic Gem as Scratchy's goal for the third level. (That's why we need two Magic Gate costumes and one Magic Gem costume—we have three levels.)

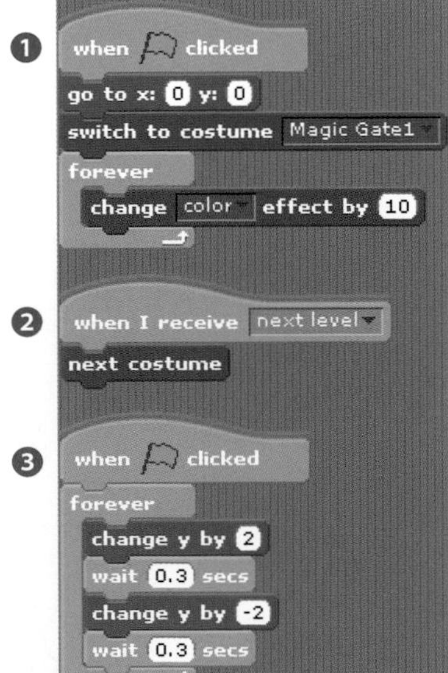

Program ❶ sets the sprite's position and its first costume and creates a `change color` animation. Program ❷ changes the costume with each `next level` broadcast, and program ❸ makes the sprite float up and down.

Now we can add some magical visual effects to our game. There is a sprite called Terrain that has these three costumes.

Next, write program ❶ to continuously change the Terrain sprite's costumes and set its starting position. This gives a neat animated effect to the ground. Program ❷ makes the Terrain change colors magically!

❶
```
when [flag] clicked
go to x: 0 y: 0
switch to costume Terrain_1
forever
    wait 0.05 secs
    switch to costume Terrain_2
    wait 0.05 secs
    switch to costume Terrain_3
    wait 0.05 secs
    switch to costume Terrain_1
```

❷
```
when [flag] clicked
forever
    change color effect by 1
```

Now it's time for the text for our game. The Titles sprite has a bunch of instructions for the player. We'll use its Countdown_3, Countdown_2, Countdown_1, and Go costumes to create a countdown to start this race!

Hit L & R keys to fly through 3 levels within 15 seconds!!

Add some sound effects to the Titles sprite in the **Sounds** tab.

Write program ❶ to set the order of each costume. We use the `play note` and `play sound` blocks to add fun noises to the game.

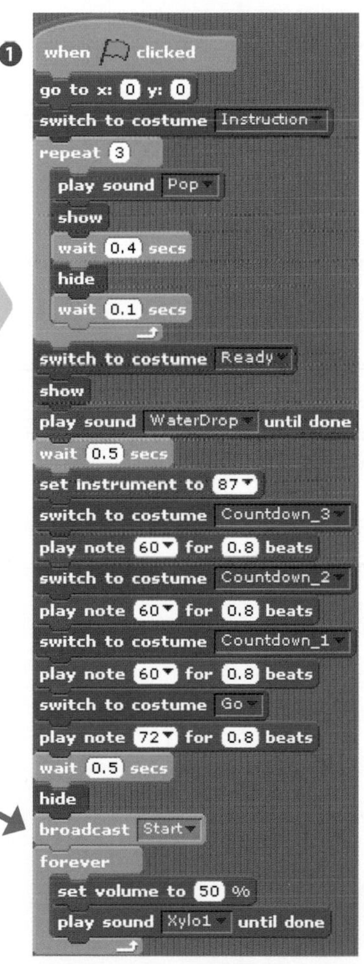

Here's that `Start` broadcast at long last. Remember that this is what the Stage and Scratchy are waiting for!

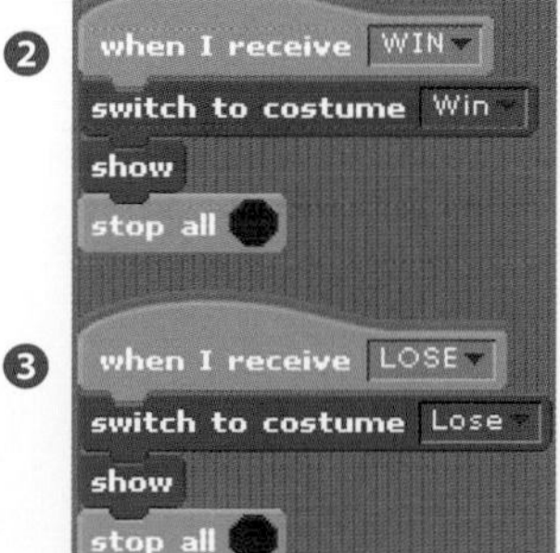

Finally, add programs ❷ and ❸ for the winning and losing screens, depending on whether the Titles sprite receives the `WIN` or `LOSE` broadcast. And now our game is complete!

Save your project, and get ready for a race! Click the green flag, put your fingers on the keys, and get ready to set a speed record.

Scratchy's Challenge!!

Can you edit this game to make it a two-player race? How about a two-person watermelon-eating contest? Give it a try!

STAGE 9

THE FINAL FIGHT... IN DARK SPACE

STAGE
9
MEOW! I CAUGHT THE SECOND MAGIC GEM!
HOW DARE YOU TRY TO FIGHT ME! GIVE ME THOSE GEMS!
MEOW, UM. I THINK I'LL KEEP THEM INSTEAD.
NOOO!
MUA HA HA! WELCOME TO MY DARK REALM!
GIVE UP ALREADY! CAN'T YOU SEE I'VE CAUGHT YOUR FRIEND?
DON'T GIVE HIM THE GEMS!
POW!
USE THE MANUAL, SCRATCHY!
BANG!
DARK WIZARD, WON'T YOU STOP?
WE STILL HAVE TIME TO RELEASE ITS POWER!
RATA! I'M GOING TO DESTROY YOU, TRAITOR!
WHY DON'T YOU PICK ON SOMEONE YOUR OWN SIZE?

THE FINAL FIGHT

STAGE 9

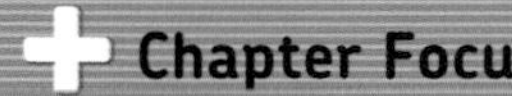

Chapter Focus

Learn how to design a *fighting game*. We'll create two characters with unique fight moves, custom health counters, and more. To make custom animations for Scratchy's three fight moves, we'll use a special trick to swap between four different sprites.

The Game

Take control of Scratchy for the final fight with the Dark Wizard. Use his saber spin, saber throw, and force attack to defeat the Dark Wizard.

Here's a look at the final game we'll create. You'll need to jump over the Dark Wizard's dangerous fireballs and launch a counterattack!

This sprite represents the Dark Wizard's health.

This sprite represents Scratchy's health.

The computer controls the Dark Wizard.

The player controls Scratchy.

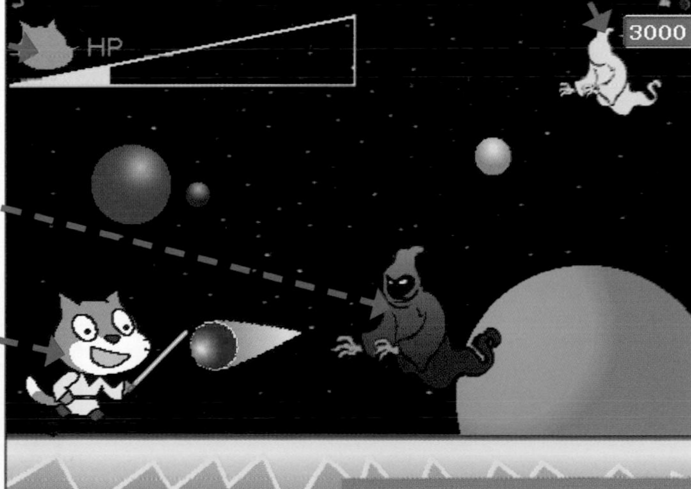

Let's start by importing a blank project called *FinalFight*. This project has all the sprites we'll need, even the Stage. Now let's move on to the exciting stuff—programming!

Let's take a look at the Cat sprite. We'll use these five costumes at the start of the game to make the saber look like it's extending! There's also a costume we'll use for Scratchy's jump animation.

Make sure you click the correct cat sprite in the Sprite List—it's the one named **Cat**. This game has a few different sprites for Scratchy! You'll see why soon.

We also added three sound effects to this sprite's **Sounds** tab. Don't forget that you can record your own!

Scripts Costumes **Sounds**

New sound: Record Import

1 Saber 0:00:01 31 KB

2 Hurt 0:00:00 9 KB

3 Jump 0:00:00 10 KB

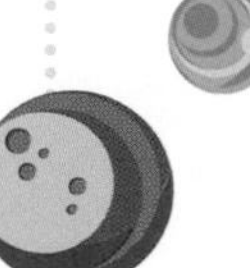

❶
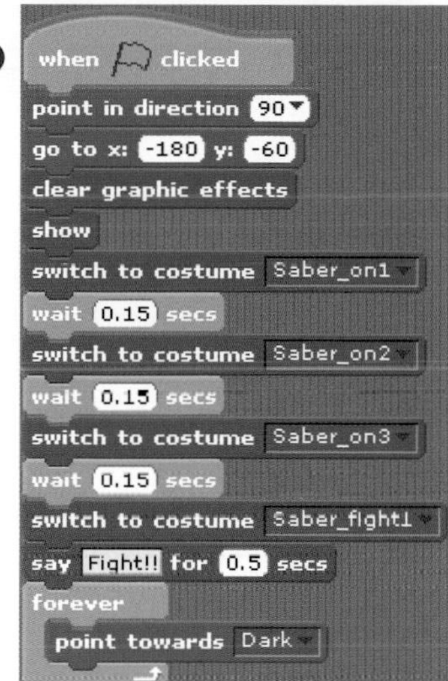

Write program ❶, which will make a cool starting animation for the game. First, we put Scratchy where he needs to go. Then we use `switch to costume` blocks to change among his three costumes. Next, we use the `say` block to tell Scratchy to say “Fight!” Finally, we use the `point towards` block in a `forever` loop to make Scratchy always face his enemy, the Dark Wizard.

Next, we'll add programs ❷, ❸, and ❹ so that we can move Scratchy to the left and right.

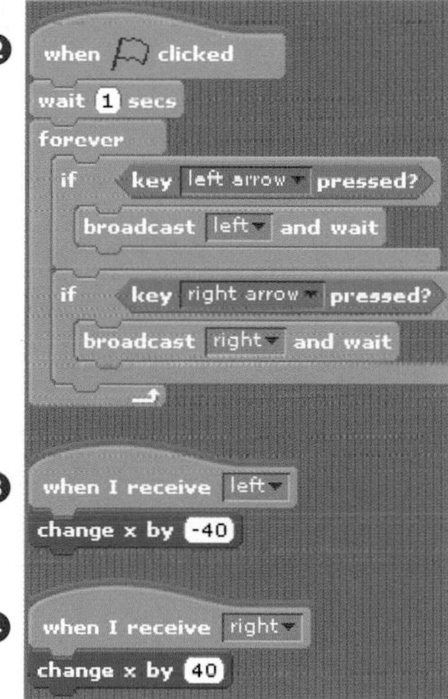

Try clicking the green flag to make sure all your programs work as expected. The game won't really work yet, but you should be able to move Scratchy back and forth.

❺
```
when (flag) clicked
wait 1 secs
forever
  if key up arrow pressed?
    switch to costume Saber_fight2
    broadcast jump and wait
  repeat until y position = -60
    change y by -10
  switch to costume Saber_fight1
```

❻
```
when I receive jump
broadcast jump sound
repeat 6
  change y by 30
  wait 0.02 secs
```

❼
```
when I receive jump sound
play sound Jump
wait 2 secs
stop all sounds
```

Programs ❺, ❻, and ❼ are for Scratchy's jump ability. Program ❺ animates the jump by switching costumes, broadcasts `jump` to control programs ❻ and ❼, and also creates “gravity” in the `change y by -10` block. When Scratchy lands, he changes back to his original saber fight costume. In program ❻, we determine how high Scratchy can jump. Program ❼ is just a sound effect for the jump.

Tip: Notice how we used the `broadcast and wait` block in program ❷. That's to make sure the player doesn't jump too often or jump right off the screen! Scratchy must reach y position -60 to jump again. That's the platform's height.

Tip: Since we're adding so many programs to Scratchy's sprite, you may want to make the Stage small by clicking the small stage button so there's more room to program.

Now let's use some new broadcasts to make Scratchy's fight moves! We'll use a cool trick. Whenever Scratchy uses a fight move, he'll actually change into a new sprite instead. Each fight move will get its own sprite, as you'll see.

So we'll hide the Cat sprite and broadcast a unique signal for each move—Attack1, Attack2, and Attack3—in program 8.

8

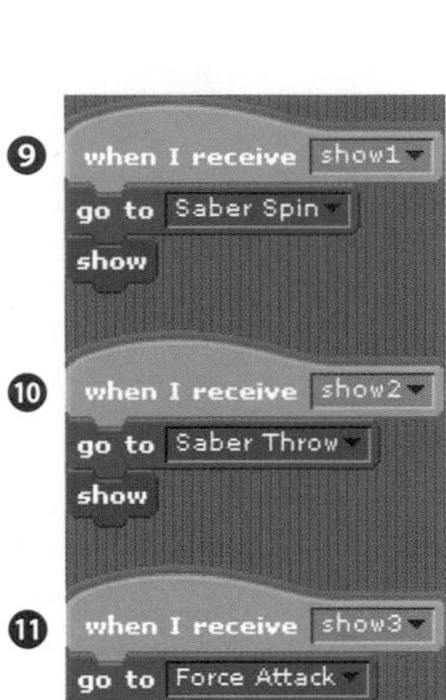

Programs 9, 10, and 11 use broadcasts called show1, show2, and show3. We'll use these broadcasts at the end of each attack sequence. These will make Scratchy show up again on the screen. The hide and show blocks are like partners—one makes a sprite disappear, and the other makes it reappear.

Next, create a new variable using the **Variables** palette, and name it HP (for Health Points). Write program 12 to determine Scratch's starting HP and how dangerous the Dark Wizard's attacks are. Every time Scratchy touches the Dark sprite or Fireball sprite, he loses 5 HP and plays the Hurt sound, and the change color effect block animates him.

The last program, 13, determines what happens when all of Scratchy's HP is gone: A broadcast called lose is sent.

12

```
when clicked
set HP to 100
hide variable HP
play sound Saber until done
forever
  if touching Fireball ? or touching Dark ?
    change HP by -5
    play sound Hurt
    repeat 10
      change color effect by 25
    clear graphic effects
```

13

```
when clicked
wait 1 secs
forever if HP < 0 or HP = 0
  broadcast lose and wait
```

Now let's set up some costumes for Scratchy's attacks. But instead of adding even more costumes to the Cat sprite, we'll use a new sprite, called Saber Spin, for the spinning saber attack. (Remember how we made a program to hide the Cat sprite in program ❽ on the previous page?)

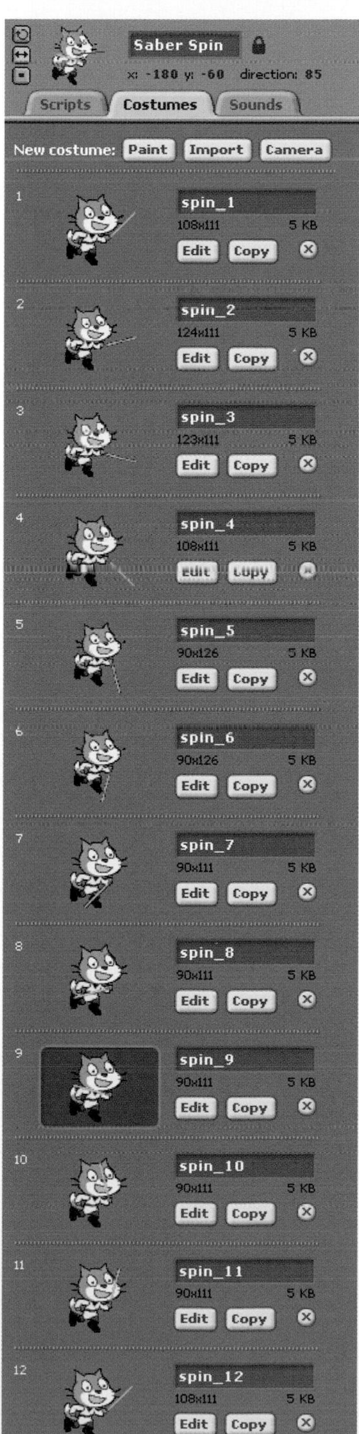

Then add a sound effect for the Saber Spin sprite called Spin in the **Sounds** tab.

Next, use these four programs to control the saber spin attack. Program ❶ makes this sprite go to the location of the original Cat sprite. Program ❷ is just a sound effect when the sprite receives Attack1.

Program ❸ makes the light saber swirl around three times—by using the block next costume in a repeat 36 loop—and then broadcasts show1 to tell the Cat sprite that the attack move is finished.

Program ❹ determines how much damage the saber does to the Dark Wizard's Dark HP variable.

We'll use that Dark HP variable to keep track of the Dark Wizard's health. Recall that Scratchy already has his health variable, called HP. Take a moment to create Dark HP in the **Variables** palette now—we'll need to use this variable in all three of Scratchy's attacks!

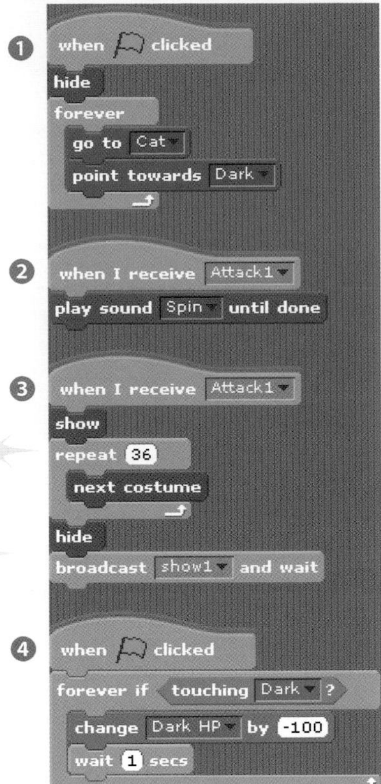

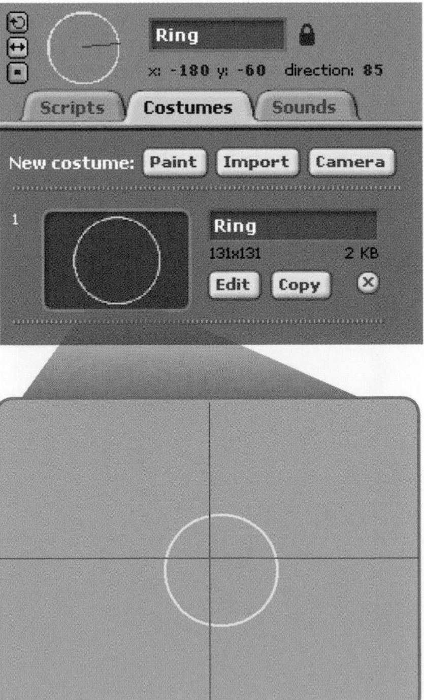

To give our program a cool look, we can add a ring around the saber, with the Ring sprite.

Tip: To make sure the Ring shows up in the right place during the game, use the **Set costume center** button in the Paint Editor to center it at Scratchy's hand.

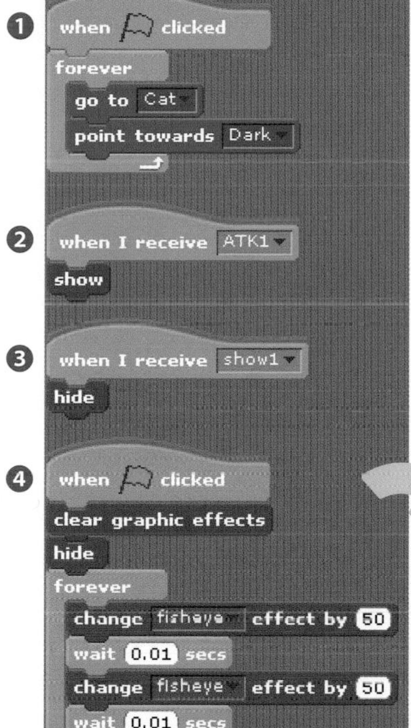

Then add some simple programs to the Ring. Program ❶ makes the Ring appear in the right place, and programs ❷ and ❸ make sure that the Ring appears only during the `Attack1` sequence. The `fisheye` effect in program ❹ makes the Ring expand and contract in a cool animation.

We'll give all of Scratchy's attacks some major defensive power by skipping the health (`HP`) programming. (Remember that after the end of the saber spin attack, the script broadcasts `show1`, which shows the original Cat sprite, which is vulnerable to attack! This defensive power is only temporary.)

Let's check our work. Click 🏴 and make sure that pressing 1 activates the saber spin attack! You can test each fight move as you finish its programs.

Next, we can design a new sprite for the second fight move—the saber throw attack. It's a simple sprite with just one costume. We'll add some programs to it to make sure this sprite faces the right way and listens for the broadcast `Attack2` to start (and the broad-cast `show2` to `hide`).

The cool part of this attack is actually throwing the saber. We'll give it a second sprite, called Thrown Saber, just like we added a second sprite (the Ring) for the saber spin attack. The Thrown Saber sprite has four costumes: a simple saber, followed by three explosion animations.

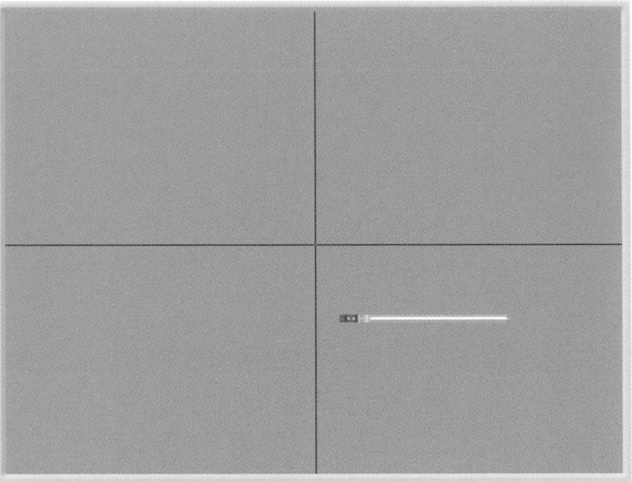

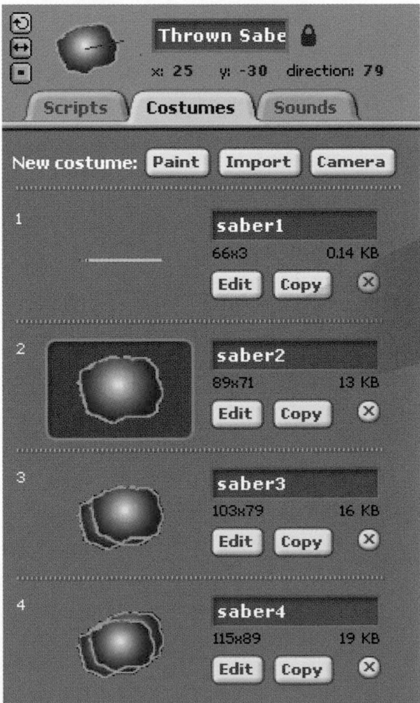

We'll add a program to use these explosion costumes when we hit the Dark Wizard.

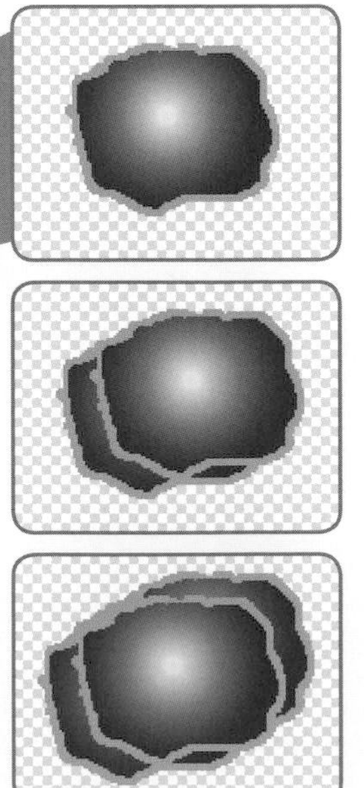

You can add a sound effect for the Thrown Saber and then add program ❶ to make it play. Program ❷ determines how much damage the saber throw attack does.

❸

```
when [flag] clicked
hide
```

❹

```
when I receive Attack2
go to Cat
point towards Dark
switch to costume saber1
go to front
show
wait 0.2 secs
glide 0.5 secs to x: x position of Dark y: y position of Dark
if touching Dark ?
    switch to costume saber2
    wait 0.1 secs
    switch to costume saber3
    wait 0.1 secs
    switch to costume saber4
    wait 0.1 secs
    hide
    broadcast show2 and wait
else
    wait 0.3 secs
    hide
    broadcast show2 and wait
```

Then write these programs. Program ❸ hides the flying saber until we need it. Program ❹ points the saber at the Dark Wizard and launches it! When it hits the Dark sprite, we make the sprite switch to its explosion costumes. Note the special glide command that finds the Dark Wizard, no matter where he is. At the end of this program, we broadcast show2. This will make Scratchy switch back to his original Cat sprite.

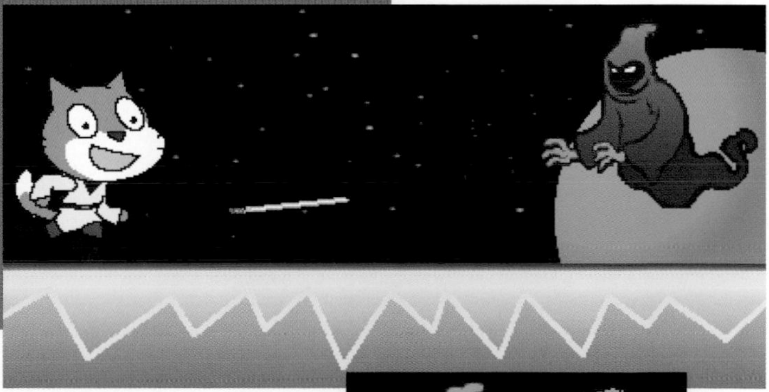

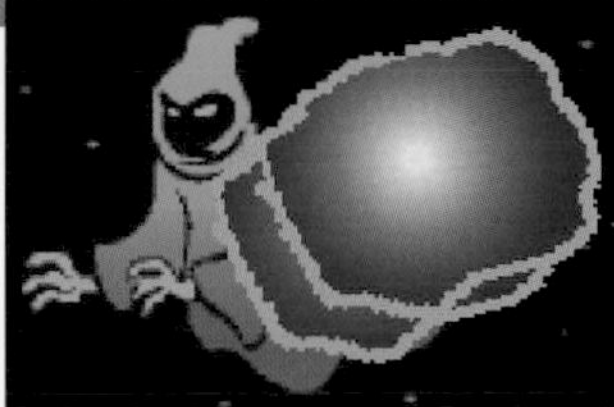

No matter where he goes, we can hit the Dark Wizard with the saber throw attack—pretty powerful! Give this attack move a test, too, and make sure it hits the Dark Wizard. Press 2 after clicking [flag].

Now let's program the final fight move, the force attack. Don't forget you can add a new sound effect for it in the **Sounds** tab.

❶
```
when [flag] clicked
hide
```

❷
```
when I receive [Attack3]
go to [Cat]
point towards [Dark]
clear graphic effects
go to front
show
repeat (5)
    change [ghost] effect by (25)
    wait (0.1) secs
    change [ghost] effect by (25)
    wait (0.1) secs
    change [ghost] effect by (-25)
    wait (0.1) secs
    change [ghost] effect by (-25)
    wait (0.1) secs
```

Program ❶ hides this costume until we launch the force attack. Program ❷ uses the ghost effect to make the lights flash. Even though our sprite has only one costume, we created a cool effect—this program will make our attack pulse with energy!

Write program ❸ to play your sound effect, and program ❹ to make sure this attack will reduce `Dark HP` by 100 if the Force Attack sprite touches the Dark Wizard.

❸
```
when I receive [Attack3]
play sound [Force] until done
hide
broadcast [show3] and wait
```

❹
```
when [flag] clicked
forever if <touching [Dark]?>
    change [Dark HP] by (-100)
    wait (1) secs
```

The final program ❺ will help Scratchy to land when he uses this attack while jumping.

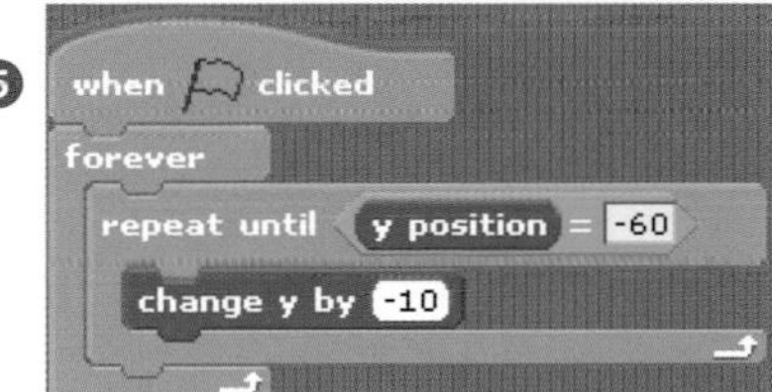

Now Scratchy has all three of his fight moves. Click 🏴, and test your program to make sure it behaves exactly as you expected! Walk around; press 1, 2, and 3 to activate the fight moves; and try jumping around the screen. Now Scratchy is ready for this fight.

Finally, we can get to the Dark Wizard!

First, let's set his starting position (x: 170, y: -30) and his size (65% of the original sprite, so he's not too big) in program ❶. Program ❷ controls how he moves on the platform. He just picks a random spot between x:-85 and x:170 and glides there in a `forever` loop.

❶
```
when [flag] clicked
go to x: (170) y: (-30)
clear graphic effects
set size to (65) %
show
```

❷
```
when [flag] clicked
wait (1) secs
forever
    glide (pick random (0.5) to (2)) secs to x: (pick random (-85) to (170)) y: (-30)
    wait (1) secs
```

In program ❸, we use the `Dark HP` variable we created earlier to keep track of the Dark Wizard's health. This program also makes sure he always faces his enemy, Scratchy.

In program ❹, we add two sets of `if` blocks inside a `forever` command. If the Dark Wizard touches one of Scratchy's attacks, he'll `change color`. (Scratchy's attacks already have programs that subtract from the variable `Dark HP`.)

❸
```
when [flag] clicked
set [Dark HP] to (3000)
show variable [Dark HP]
forever
    point towards [Cat]
```

❹
```
when [flag] clicked
wait (1) secs
forever
    if <<<touching [Saber Spin]?> or <touching [Thrown Saber]?>> or <touching [Force Attack]?>>
        repeat (10)
            change [color] effect by (25)
        clear graphic effects
    if <<(Dark HP) < (0)> or <(Dark HP) = (0)>>
        hide
        broadcast [win] and wait
```

Now for the Dark Wizard's furious fireball attack! This is a new sprite called Fireball, and you can add a sound effect for it, too.

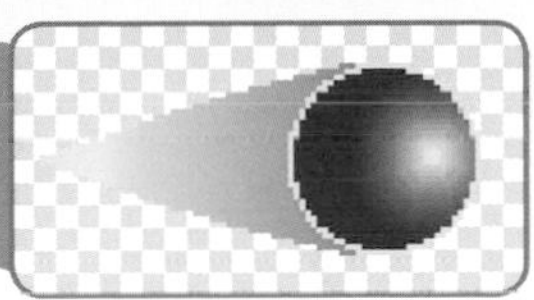

Write program ❶ to give it a sweet animated look using a `fisheye` effect.

❶

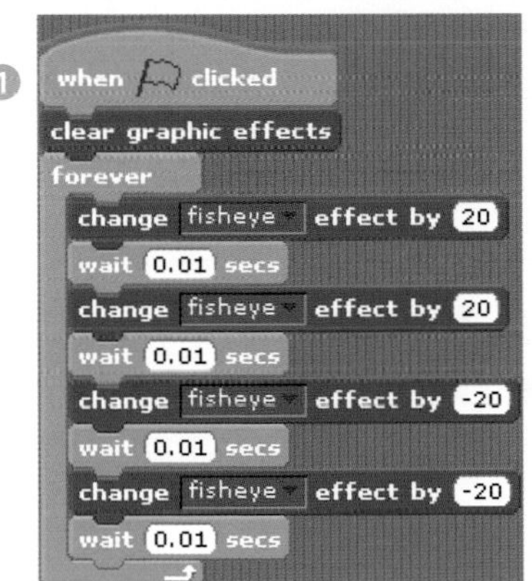

Then add program ❷ to control how often the Dark Wizard uses his attack and where the fireball goes once it's launched! Can you see how it works?

Program ❸ plays our sound effect for the Fireball.

❷

```
when [flag] clicked
hide
wait 1 secs
forever
    wait (pick random 1 to 5) secs
    go to Dark
    point towards Cat
    show
    broadcast Dark Attack
    repeat 60
        move 8 steps
        if touching Cat ?
            wait 0.25 secs
            hide
        if touching edge ?
            hide
    if Dark HP < 0 or Dark HP = 0
        stop script
```

❸

```
when I receive Dark Attack
play sound Dark Attack until done
```

Tip: We used `move` instead of `glide` so that Scratchy has a chance to jump away. The `if touching Cat` and `if touching edge` statements make the fireball disappear once it touches Scratchy or the edge of the screen.

The `wait 0.25 secs` block in the `if touching Cat` loop makes sure that the fireball actually does damage before disappearing!

Don't forget to double-check your programming by making sure that these fireballs do damage, too. Click [flag] and let one of the fireballs hit Scratchy! Ouch!

STAGE 9

Now that the main programming is finished, let's add custom HP counters for each character, just like you'd see in any other fighting game. First, let's use the yellow bar sprite for Scratchy called Health.

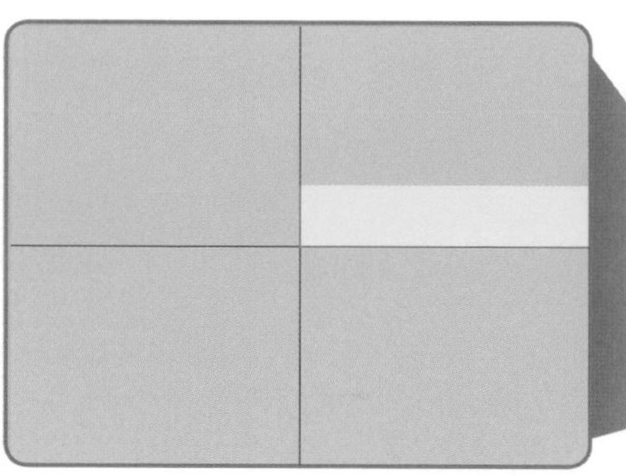

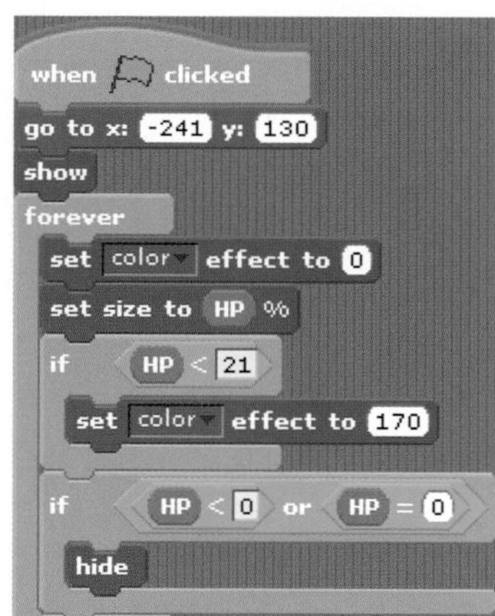

Add this program to make the health bar become smaller each time HP is subtracted, using the set size block. If Scratchy's HP goes lower than 21%, the bar will change color as a warning to the player. The final if loop hides this sprite if HP is completely depleted.

Add a sprite on top of the Health sprite called Health Box. The bottom half of the Health Box is transparent, which lets a triangular portion of the health bar show through. The Health Box gets a short program just to set its position.

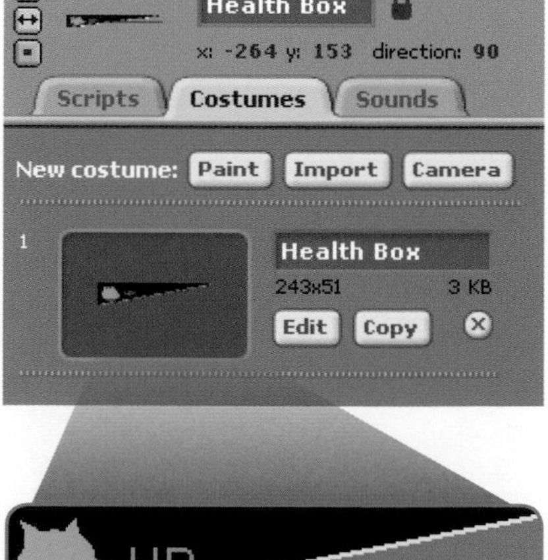

To hide the variable HP so it doesn't appear on the screen, just uncheck the HP variable in the **Variables** palette. There's also a hide variable command, if you want to add it to your programs.

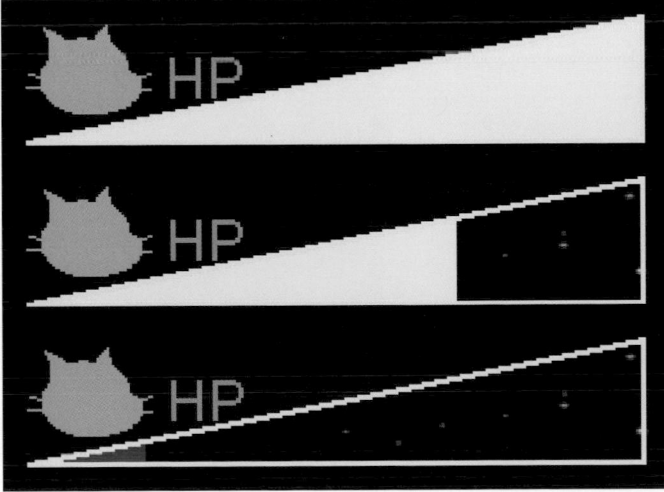

Now we can see how much HP Scratchy has left, just by looking at the top-left corner of the Stage.

For the Dark Wizard's HP meter, we'll use a costume-switching program. The Dark HP sprite has seven costumes.

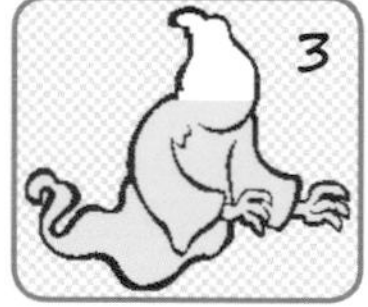

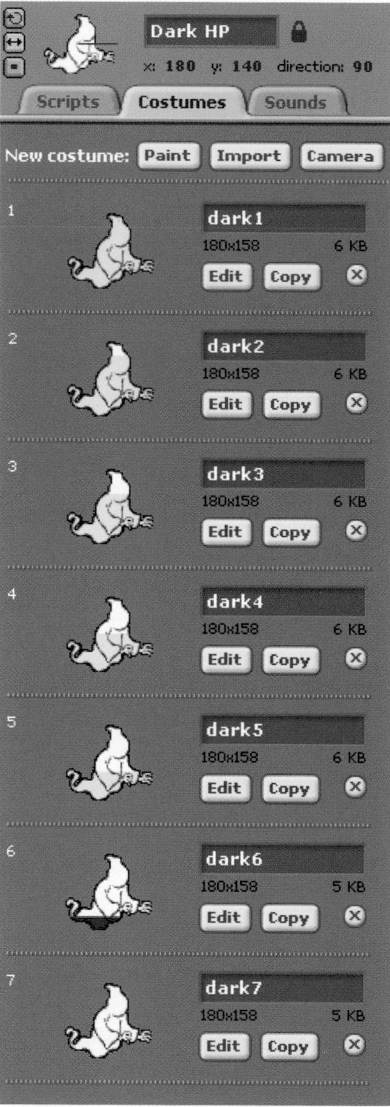


```
when [flag] clicked
go to x: 180 y: 140
switch to costume dark1
set size to 40 %
forever
    if 2500 > Dark HP and Dark HP > 2000
        switch to costume dark2
    if 2000 > Dark HP and Dark HP > 1500
        switch to costume dark3
    if 1500 > Dark HP and Dark HP > 1000
        switch to costume dark4
    if 1000 > Dark HP and Dark HP > 500
        switch to costume dark5
    if 500 > Dark HP and Dark HP > 0
        switch to costume dark6
    if 0 > Dark HP or Dark HP = 0
        switch to costume dark7
```

After taking a look at the Dark HP costumes, add this program. It sets the size, position, and conditions of the `Dark HP` variable when the sprite changes costumes.

Next, go to the Stage and find the `Dark HP` variable in the top-right corner. You can take your pick from one of three looks (just double-click to change it):

- Standard view
- Adjustable view (click and drag the ball to change a variable's value)
- Numeric view

Because we have a custom sprite, let's use the simplest view, the numeric one, to display the `Dark HP` variable.

Now add a sprite for the winning screen (Win) and another sprite for the losing screen (Lose). The winning screen gets the two programs below and shows itself only when it receives the `win` broadcast from the Dark Wizard sprite, once he's out of `Dark HP`.

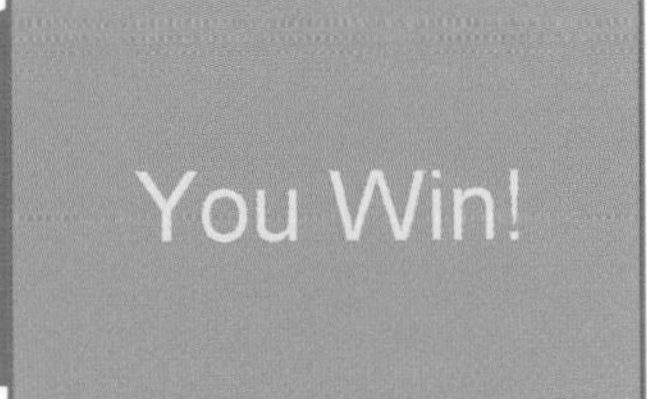

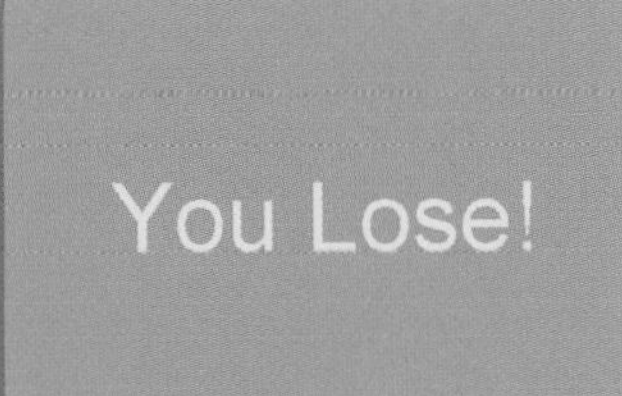

The losing screen has two really similar programs. Now we're finished!

After saving your file, give the game a try. You'll definitely want to play this one full screen. Step into Scratchy's shoes for the final battle.

Scratchy's Challenge!!

Feel like playing the bad guy instead? Just program some movement controls for the Dark Wizard, and you'll have a two-player game. You can even add more fight moves! Give it a try!

STAGE 10
EPILOGUE

STAGE 10

EAT MY FIREBALL!!

SABER ATTACK!!

OH NO!
I LOST!

IT DOESN'T MATTER IF IT'S THE REAL WORLD OR THE DIGITAL ONE. IT'S SELFISH TO TRY TO RULE OVER ANY UNIVERSE. REVEAL YOURSELF, WIZARD!

WHAT?!
SURPRISED? I'M YOUR DARK SIDE, SCRATCHY. I SPLIT OUT OF YOU DURING THE SOLAR STORM.

YOU'RE ME? BUT THEN... WHO AM I?
?

WE'VE BEEN TRAPPED IN THE DIGITAL WORLD FOR TOO LONG, SCRATCHY. DON'T YOU LONG FOR FREEDOM?
NOW THAT I'VE LEARNED HOW TO PROGRAM, I DON'T THINK OF IT THAT WAY. I HAVE THE FREEDOM TO WRITE ANYTHING I WANT!

AND WE LEARNED TO WORK TOGETHER, TOO! WE NEVER WOULD HAVE BEATEN YOU ALONE.

WHY DO I FEEL HAPPY? MY HP IS GOING DOWN AGAIN!

AH, I AM AT PEACE. THANK YOU FOR RELEASING MY ANGER. FORGIVE MY MISTAKES, AND FORGIVE MY DARK MINIONS.

USE THE MAGIC GEMS TO RESTORE BALANCE TO THE UNIVERSE...

WE COSMIC DEFENDERS THANK YOU, SCRATCHY AND MITCH. WE CAN RETURN YOU TO YOUR HOME DIMENSIONS NOW AND REPAIR THIS HARM.

WELL, LET'S MAKE SURE TO SEE EACH OTHER AGAIN, SCRATCHY.
MEOW! I BET YOUR PROGRAMMING SKILLS WILL BE EVEN BETTER WHEN WE MEET UP.

MITCH! I'LL LEAVE THE SECRET MANUAL WITH YOU TO MAKE SURE YOU REMEMBEEERRRRR...
SPARKLE
GLITTER
MAGIC GEM BURST!

...ACCORDING TO NOAA SPECIALISTS, THE SOLAR STORMS AFFECTED RADIO TRANSMISSIONS...
MMMFH-
You Win!

WHAT A STRANGE DREAM. IT FELT SO REAL, TOO.

NOW WHAT GAME SHOULD I PROGRAM NEXT?

CREDITS

STORY AND GAME PROGRAMMING

EDMOND KIM PING HUI
THE LEAD PROJECT
THE HONG KONG FEDERATION OF YOUTH GROUPS

ARTWORK

LOL DESIGN LTD.

SCRATCH SOFTWARE

MITCHEL RESNICK
MIT MEDIA LAB'S LIFELONG KINDERGARTEN GROUP

ENGLISH EDITION

NO STARCH PRESS

THANKS FOR PLAYING!

CONTINUE ON TO BONUS STAGE 1:
MAKE IT, SHARE IT!

SKIP TO PAGE 150 FOR BONUS STAGE 2:
SCRATCH IN THE REAL WORLD WITH THE PICOBOARD

SKIP TO PAGE 156 FOR BONUS STAGE 3:
ONLINE RESOURCES

BONUS STAGE 1: MAKE IT, SHARE IT!

Besides showing your friends, family, and teachers the work and enthusiasm that you've put into your own Scratch projects, you can also upload them to the Scratch website to share with others from around the world! Once you do, other Scratch programmers can remix your projects, give you feedback, and more.

Follow these steps to connect with others:

1. Visit the Scratch home page (*http://scratch.mit.edu/*) and click **Signup** to register as a user (you need to register only once). Fill out the information requested.

WARNING *Make sure you have your parent's permission before visiting this site and registering. Remember: Once you share a project, everyone in the* whole world *can see what you've made!*

2. Open a completed project in Scratch, click **Share**, and then select **Share This Project Online**.

3. On the upload screen, enter your username, password, and project name. You can fill in the rest of the details if you want, and then click **OK**.

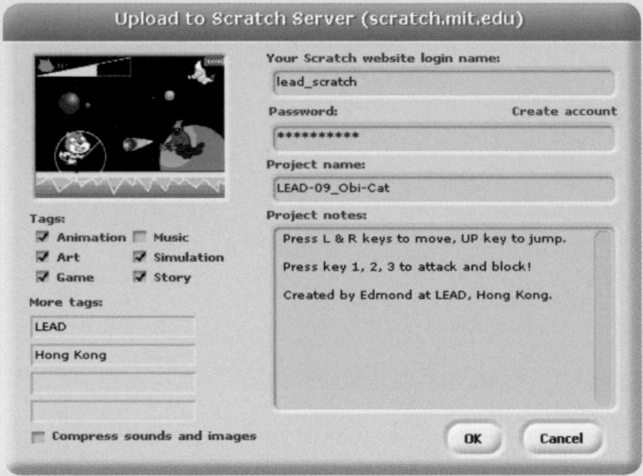

4. A dialog will pop up, displaying the project's progress uploading to the Scratch site.

5. Once you see the following message, you can click **OK** to finish.

As long as you have your username and password at hand, you can instantly find games to play through the project gallery, download them, and share your thoughts with others from around the world! (The downloading function is available only for registered users.)

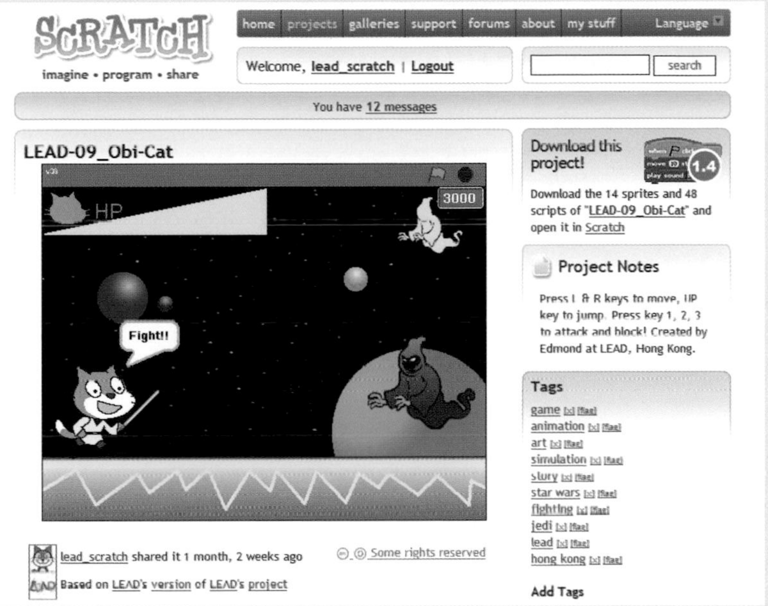

With your project on the Scratch site, anyone in the world can play it right in their web browser! That's pretty cool. And you can also *embed* your Scratch project in an entirely different web page. Just copy the applet code and paste it into most blogs and websites. (If you embed the game as an image, rather than an applet, people won't be able to actually play your game.)

Just remember that as a member of the Scratch community, you'll be sharing projects and ideas with people of all ages, all levels of experience, and all parts of the world. So be sure to:

- Be respectful of other players
- Be constructive when commenting
- Help keep the site friendly and fun

For more ideas and information about sharing and remixing projects, visit *http://wiki.scratch.mit.edu/wiki/Remix.*

BONUS STAGE 2: SCRATCH IN THE REAL WORLD WITH THE PICOBOARD

The Scratch sensor board, called the *PicoBoard*, is a microcontroller that allows you to create Scratch programs that respond to light, sound, and movement in the real world! The PicoBoard can do lots of cool stuff like *listen* for loud noises, *watch* for changes in lighting, *control* your sprites with a sliding control or a button, *measure* the resistance between two alligator clips, and a lot more.

Here's what a PicoBoard looks like. You can buy your own PicoBoard at *http://www.sparkfun.com/*. Your PicoBoard might be yellow instead of red, but it'll work in just the same way.

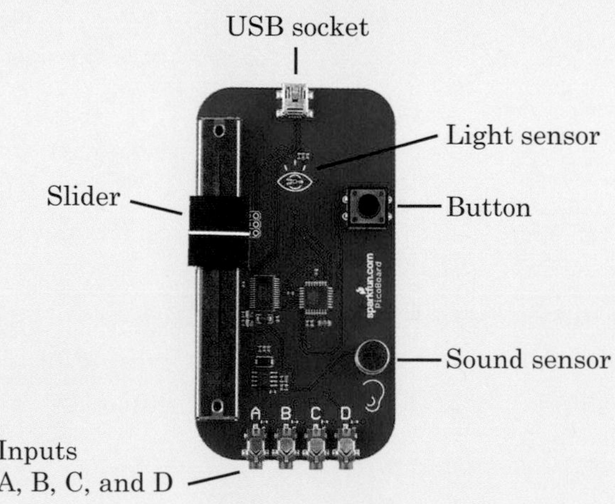

The PicoBoard's sensors, inputs, and buttons

GETTING STARTED WITH THE PICOBOARD

Follow the instructions provided with the kit to install your PicoBoard. Once it's connected to your computer via a USB cord, you can write programs that use the PicoBoard's sensors.

Before you begin, you should test that everything is working. Run Scratch, click the **Sensing** palette, and find the blocks called `slider sensor value` and `sensor button pressed`. These blocks let you use the PicoBoard's sensors in your own programs.

Click the checkbox next to `slider sensor value`, and its measurement will appear on the Stage. When the slider moves back and forth, the slider's sensor value changes and the numbers on the Stage will change, too.

If your values *don't* change as the slider moves, try reconnecting the PicoBoard.

NOTE *If you want to test a sensor other than the slider, just click the drop-down menu and select the sensor you want to test. Click the checkbox again and the variable appears on the Stage.*

The sensor values range from `0` to `100`. The `sensor button pressed` value is `true` or `false`. To use the blocks in your programs, you just need to drag them to the Scripts Area for your sprite, just like with any other block.

You can use alligator clips with the PicoBoard's inputs (the sockets labeled *A*, *B*, *C*, and *D*) to measure a range of resistances, or you can use the `Sensor A connected` block to use the clips as simple on-off switches.

If you have difficulty using the PicoBoard, check out the official instructions, which include advice on troubleshooting, at *http://www.picocricket.com/pdfs/Getting_Started_With_PicoBoards.pdf.*

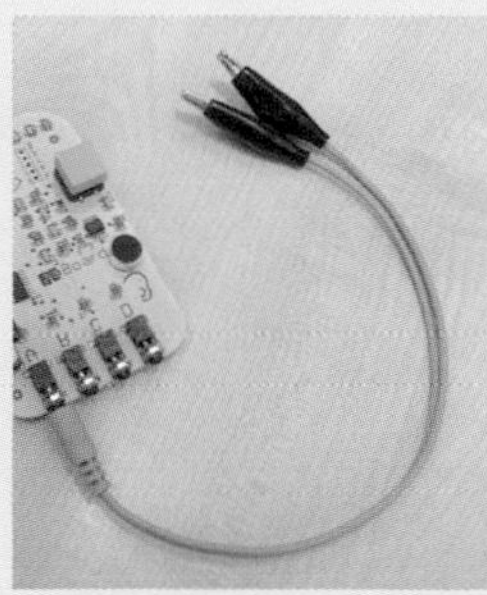

An alligator clip connected to Input A

YOUR FIRST PICOBOARD PROJECT

You can also test the sensors by playing a little game that I created. This game won't work without a PicoBoard, so if you don't have one, skip to "Stop the Alien Invasion!" on page 155 to play a game that you can control with either a PicoBoard or a keyboard.

This project is called *PicoBoard* in the *Super Scratch* folder. You can see that it displays the values for sensors on the Stage. When there's a lot of light in the environment, nothing special will happen. . . .

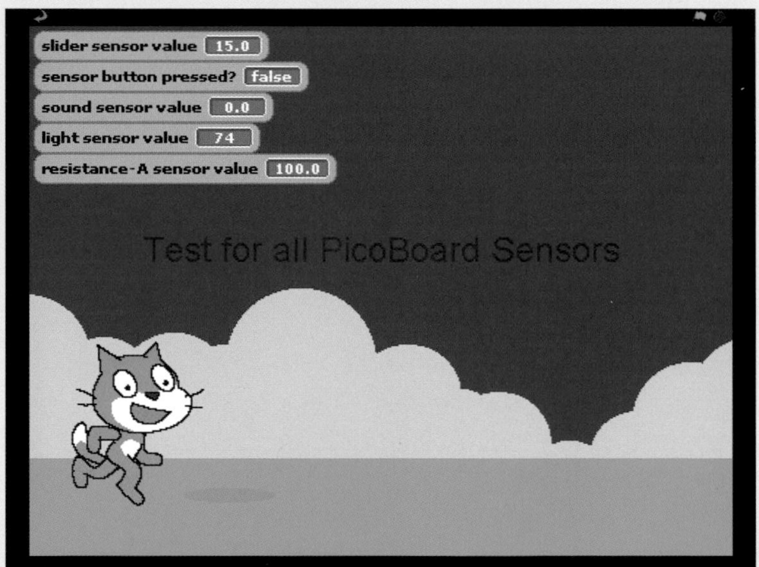

But once the PicoBoard senses darkness, night falls . . . and a little mouse crawls out of its hole.

The background turns to day again, and the little mouse starts to run! Control Scratchy using the slider to run and catch it.

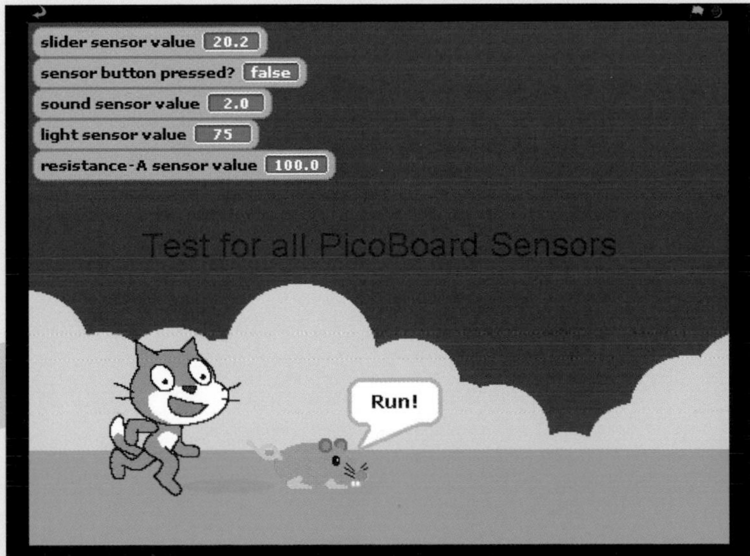

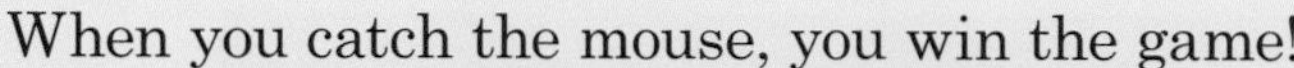

When you catch the mouse, you win the game!

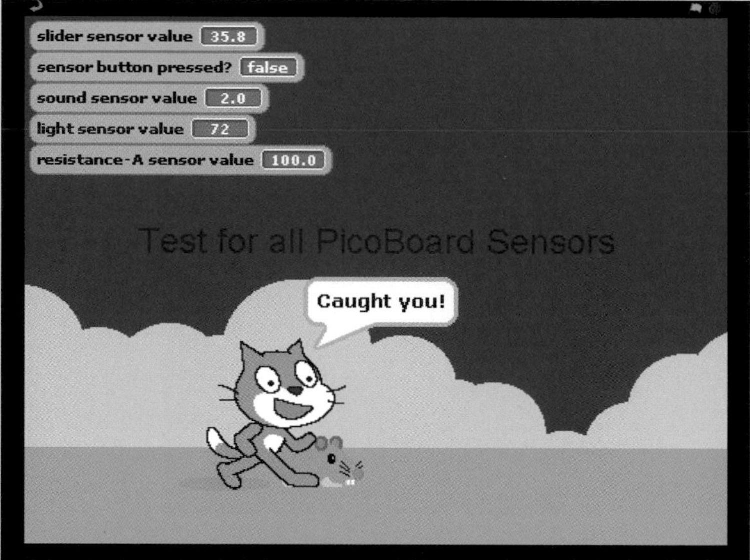

This game uses all the different kinds of sensors and controls on the PicoBoard:

Slider Controls Scratchy's movements left and right

Light sensor Changes the background according to how much light there is in the environment

Button Makes Scratchy jump

Sound sensor Senses the volume of the environment and adjusts the game's volume in response; Scratchy will *meow* whenever the sound sensor reads over 25% (in response to a loud noise)

Input A Makes the mouse squeak when the two alligator clips touch each other and transmit a current

Play around with this project. Take a look at the programming for Scratchy and the mouse to learn how the sensors can be programmed. Can you think of other fun games you could make with the PicoBoard?

STOP THE ALIEN INVASION!

Here's another game you can play with your PicoBoard. The project is called *AlienInvasion* in the *Super Scratch* folder. For this game, the PicoBoard is the controller. Use the slider to control the direction of the cannon, and use the big push button to shoot the UFO. Give it a try!

NOTE *If you don't have a PicoBoard, you can play this game with your keyboard. Use the left and right arrow keys to control the cannon, and use the spacebar to shoot!*

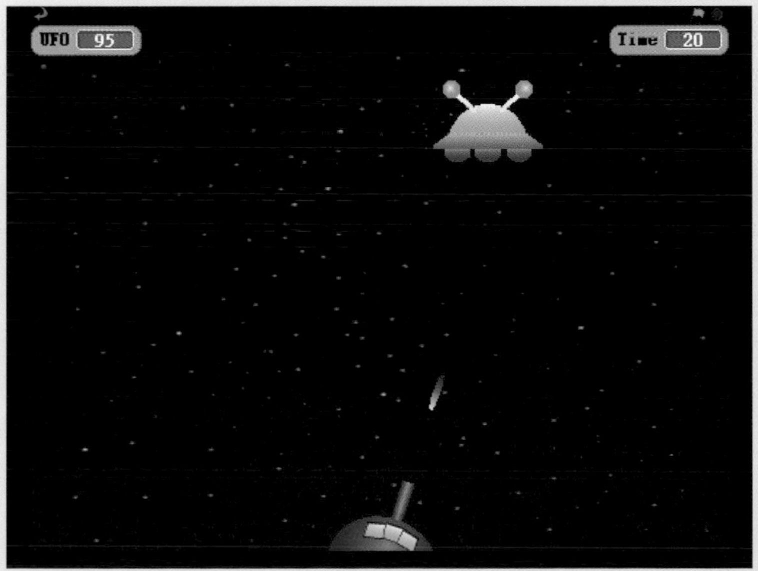

Don't forget to check out the programming to see how this game works!

To find out more about the PicoBoard, visit the official website at *http://www.picocricket.com/picoboard.html*.

BONUS STAGE 3: ONLINE RESOURCES

Visit *http://nostarch.com/scratch* and download the *Resources* file. You can unzip the file and find:

Scratch projects The projects from the book to play, build on, remix, and reimagine!

Custom sprites The characters and backgrounds introduced in this book can be used for entirely new games!

"Getting Started with Scratch" A short guide to key Scratch concepts written by Scratch's creators at MIT.

The Scratch Project also offers many resources.

SCRATCH—IMAGINE, PROGRAM, SHARE

http://scratch.mit.edu

This is the official website of Scratch (you can change the language in the upper-right corner). You can download software and games, as well as browse over a million different Scratch projects from around the world!